Bob Bondurant on
HIGH PERFORMANCE
DRIVING

Completely Revised & Updated
With New Technology For The 1990s

Bob Bondurant
With John Blakemore

Motorbooks International
Publishers & Wholesalers ®

I would like to thank the following people for their assistance in making this book possible: Linda Muncey of the Bondurant school; Mari Stefonetti and Refractions of Albany; Eastman Kodak Company; Wolfgang Scholvien; Connie, John, and Rebecca Kämpfe; Lisa Mower; Canon Cameras; Miguel Caparros and Eurocar International; Troy Amos; Rick Dickerson; Bart Davis; Dave Preston; Carolyn Sweeney and Going Places Travel; Pamela Lauesen and George Goad of the Formula 1 Spectators Association; Bruce Trenery and Fantasy Junction; Calvin Chang and Snap-on Tools; Tim Parker and Michael Dregni of Motorbooks International.

John Blakemore
Emeryville, California

First published in 1993 by Motorbooks International Publishers & Wholesalers, PO Box 2, 729 Prospect Avenue, Osceola, WI 54020 USA

Motorbooks International is a certified trademark, registered with the United States Patent Office

The information in this book is true and complete to the best of our knowledge. All recommendations are made without any guarantee on the part of the author or Publisher, who also disclaim any liability incurred in connection with the use of this data or specific details

We recognize that some words, model names and designations, for example, mentioned herein are the property of the trademark holder. We use them for identification purposes only. This is not an official publication

Motorbooks International books are also available at discounts in bulk quantity for industrial or sales-promotional use. For details write to Special Sales Manager at the Publisher's address

Library of Congress Cataloging-in-Publication Data

Bondurant, Bob.
    Bob Bondurant on high performance driving/Bob Bondurant with John Blakemore – –3rd ed.
        p. cm.
        Includes bibliographical references (p.) and index.
        ISBN 0-879380751-3
    1. Automobile racing. 2. Automobile driving. I. Blakemore, John. II. Title.
    GV1029.B673 1993
    796.7'2– –dc20   93-15681

On the front cover: Ford 5.0 liter V-8 Mustangs working through the new course of the Bob Bondurant School of High Performance Driving at Firebird International Raceway, Phoenix, Arizona. *John Blakemore*

Printed and bound in the United States of America

Contents

Acknowledgments

I want to thank the following people who, through the sport of motor racing, made my life possible as it is today.

My late cousin, J. C. Lewis, who introduced me to sports car road racing in 1955.

The late Don Bechtold, for his loyalty, enthusiasm and hard work in race-preparing my #285x Indian 101 Scout in 1951 and then our famous #51 orange Corvette. You helped me win the SCCA B-Production Championship and Valvoline's Best Corvette Driver of the Year in 1959 by winning eighteen out of twenty races.

Shelly Washburn and Bob Joehnck of Santa Barbara, California, who owned one of the most immaculate race-prepared Corvettes in the country. I enjoyed winning races with you both. Shelly, I want to thank you for my first pro ride.

Marie, my third wife, who gave me the encouragement and support to go professional racing with Carroll Shelby in Europe.

Carroll Shelby, for your confidence in me. Thank you for letting me race and test drive your famous Cobras, King Cobras, Daytonas, and GT 40s. Carroll, you gave me my real break that launched my professional career and all that has come after. Thank you for giving me the opportunity of working in your racing school,

teaching James Garner and the others for the movie *Grand Prix*. That fulfilling experience was the spark that, coupled with my 150mph accident, started the Bob Bondurant School of High Performance Driving, on February 14, 1968.

Leo Mehl, Bob Toth, Andy Kunos, and the entire Goodyear Racing Staff from 1963 on. You have been a greater help than you could ever imagine. Thanks again for your continued support of the Bondurant school and for your support of our new and on-going Bondurant Driver PROSearch to send our best young driver to the Trans Am series.

Many thanks to Phil Hill for all of your help at my first European race at the Targa Florio as your co-driver in Shelby's 289 Cobra. We did lead until the halfshaft broke. Thanks for your help and continued friendship over the years.

Jackie Stewart, for all of your help in this great sport and as a valued friend. I enjoyed training your son, Paul, who is really coming into his own and driving great in single-seaters today. I'm proud of him as a Bondurant Racing Graduate.

The late Graham Hill, for all of his help at the Nürburgring and the other circuits around the world of Formula 1. All the best to his beautiful and supportive wife, Bette, and son, Damon, who is heading the right direction in Formula 1.

The late Jimmy Clark, a truly great champion, for all of his personal help and encouragement.

The late Enzo Ferrari, for giving me my first Formula 1 ride at the US Grand Prix in 1965 and a contract to drive Ferrari prototypes for all of the 1966 season.

Ken ("Chopper") Tyrrell, for giving me that real driver's test at Goodwood in 1965 in your Cooper Formula 3 car. I was pleased that I was almost as fast as Jackie Stewart and you let me drive the Monaco Formula 3 race. Thanks for teaching me how to really qualify by staying out to the last lap and running as fast as I could. It paid off as we set a new lap record, a full second faster than second-place Roy Pike. I also really enjoyed driving your Formula 2 Cooper teamed with Jackie.

John Frankenheimer, for hiring me to work on the movie *Grand Prix* and training James Garner, Yves Montand, Brian Bedford, and Antonio Sabato. What a great new and rewarding experience that was.

Bernard White, for my 1966 season and my first full Grand Prix ride in your 2.0 liter BRM Formula 1 GP car.

Dan Gurney, for doing such a great job at the 1964 Le Mans 24 Hour race. I was incredibly proud to be your co-driver, winning the GT Category and placing fourth overall. Thanks Dan for my drives in your fantastic Eagle Formula 1 cars in the US and Mexican Grands Prix in 1966. I have really enjoyed our long-term friendship. More recently it was great giving you a refresher course at my school for your NASCAR ride. What great fun!

Paul Newman, for sponsoring me in my Can-Am rides. I'm proud to have trained you in my school for your fantastic racing career. You're super to work with!

And a great race driver!

Robert Wagner, I enjoyed training you and Paul for the movie *Winning*. Remember the Lola T-70 at Elkhart Lake in Turn Four? I'm glad I made you drive it again, aren't you?

Bernard and Joanie Cahier, for all of your gracious help and thoughts throughout my entire European racing career. Some things just don't change. Thanks for the great friendship even today.

Graham Warner of Checkered Flag Racing, London, for giving me rides early each session in Formula 3 and in the 427 Cobra that David Piper and I drove to win the Rothmans 500-mile race in the pouring rain at Brands Hatch in 1965.

Bobby, my son, for helping in the pits on several of my NASCAR rides and the IMSA races. We both like to give each other support in our racing. Congratulations on all of your wins in both the Datsun 610 in showroom stock and the orange Camaro. And now, for your growth and love of our family business. It makes my heart grow warm to help and watch you grow.

Willment Racing, outside of London, for letting me drive that Lotus Can-Am car to second place at Silverstone, behind Denny Hulme, and for giving me the car to win the Formula 3 race at Monza in 1966.

To all of our celebrities, including Paul Newman, Robert Wagner, James Garner, Paul Williams, Clint Eastwood, James Brolin, Gene Hackman, Candice Bergen, Kent McCord, John Schneider, Bill Shatner, Fred Dryer, Kitty O'Neil, John Chancellor, James Coburn, Lee Majors, Larry Wilcox, Bruce Jenner, Robert Hays, Parker Stevenson, Tommy Lee Jones, John Frankenheimer, Christopher Cross, Craig

Virgin, Ken Takakura, Yves Montand, Elke Sommer, Tom Cruise, and many more. I have enjoyed all of you. Many thanks and great success to you all!

I especially want to thank all of the special sponsors that my school has had over the last few decades: Nissan/Datsun for getting my school started and for their many years of belief and support. Porsche for its help and support during the Ontario years. Valvoline for over fifteen years of trouble-free lubrication. Champion spark plugs for the many years of great service. Bell helmets and safety equipment, Centerline wheels, H&M, and John and Mike at the Downey tire center for building all of those Bandag Racing retreads.

Additionally, I want to give special thanks to Donald Petersen, of the Ford Motor Company, "Red" Poling, David Scott and Edsel Ford II, for listening and believing in me personally and for their continued commitment, along with Bob Rewey and Gary Nielsen.

Many thanks to my loyal and enthusiastic staff who make up our wonderful school. They really have ensured that the Bondurant School is of the highest quality and have definitely made us the number-one high-performance driving school in the world through out the last twenty-five years.

I want to thank the racetrack owners and managers who have helped me around the world, including Les Richter and Roy Hoard of the Riverside Raceway; Skip Berg and the entire staff at Sears Point International Raceway; Lee Mosel of Laguna Seca; Lee Hall of Elkhart Lake; Bill France Sr. and Bill France Jr. and their entire staff at Daytona International Speedway. Additionally my thanks goes out to Charlie Mendez of Sebring Raceway; John Cooper and Ray Dmartus of The Ontario Motor Speedway. In Europe I would like to thank the organizers of the famous Targa Florio and the late Masten Gregory, the American who taught me this circuit and taught me how to learn all of the race circuits. The organizers of Goodwood, Brands Hatch, and Silverstone in England. Le Mans, Reims, Rouen, Alby, Pau in France. Nürburgring, Freiburg hill climb in Germany. Monza in Italy, Spa in Belgium, Sierra Montand in Switzerland, and Monaco—and all of the organizers for all of their help.

Most of all I would like to thank all of my current sponsors for helping me and the Bob Bondurant School of High Performance Driving reach, maintain and continue our goal of excellence: Ford Motor Company and Lincoln-Mercury for their excellent high-performance cars and trucks. Motorcraft parts and Ford Electronics for great service and reliability. Goodyear for its Eagle tires with fantastic traction, smooth ride, and predictable car control. Simpson safety equipment for making motor racing safer each day. Recaro for the best in seating. Texaco for the best in high-performance fuel and lubrication. Ronal Wheels for super-strong and beautiful lightweight wheels. Koni shocks for the best in handling and ride.

A special note of thanks to Charlie Allen and the entire staff at our new home at Firebird International Raceway, Phoenix, Arizona. It is really great to be here.

A special thanks to all of our wonderful graduates from all around the world who have helped make our school what it is today. Without you we couldn't have done it. Thank you one and all.

Bob Bondurant
Phoenix, Arizona

1

Getting Acquainted

The Bob Bondurant School of High Performance Driving is one of the most successful high-performance driving schools in the world and is owned and operated by Bob Bondurant. Bob's school, which first opened its gates to students in 1968, is world famous for being the most advanced and intense school for high-performance driving, racing, law enforcement and corporate anti-terrorist training. Bob's school not only teaches the amateur enthusiast and the aspiring racer but also the advanced professional how to perfect and improve his or her driving form.

Under the close supervision of Bondurant and his hand-picked staff, many novice would-be racers, famous personalities, and some formidable names in professional racing have passed through the gates of the Bondurant School. Some students take the school as a starter course, others a refresher, and for some it is just a "tune-up" in their driving styles. Just some of the names that Bob has given his personal instruction to are: Davy Allison, Candice Bergen, Tom Cruise, Clint East-

wood, Bill Elliott, James Garner, Gene Hackman, Lori Johns, Perry King, Rick Mears, Paul Newman, Elke Sommer, and Al Unser, Jr.—just to name a few. Not too long ago, Bob also had the pleasure of giving a refresher course to Dan Gurney, his old Cobra racing teammate.

As well as earning the respect of the racing fraternity, Bob and his school are number one in the world of street driving. The Bondurant School also offers the world's best courses in two highly specialized areas. For the last twenty years, Bob has had a special academy for instructing law-enforcement officers in the proper techniques of handling their police cars in nearly all situations, including pursuit.

Bob's other special course is what he refers to as his "Executive Protection" course. This one deals with executives, VIPs, and their chauffeurs, teaching them how to get away from would-be terrorists and kidnappers. All of Bob's courses deal with reality. The actuality of the how, and the why and then many hours behind the wheel practicing to ensure that it is all un-

Dan Gurney and I had a fun two days at my school during his "refresher" course before his NASCAR comeback in 1980.... He sure hadn't lost his touch.

derstood and done correctly.

Bob's credentials are enough, in themselves, to fill a book. It is only right that we take a few quick laps through the pages that brought Bob Bondurant into the world of high-performance driving instruction. Over 2,500 students per year attend the Bondurant School's various driving courses.

Bob's first interest in racing was sparked when he was eight years old, watching midget dirt-track oval racers with his father. It wasn't long until, at the age of 14, he was riding a Whizzer motorbike, and then motorcycle racing an Indian 101 Scout on the dirt-track ovals in Southern California. Next it was hot-rodding and informal drag racing, then finally his first road-racing car. Bob shares some of his reflections of his early days of competition—and, along with those thoughts, one can see how he molded and formed his concepts of how to teach others to drive both quicker and safer:

The days of motorcycle racing, mo-tocross, and the ovals like the mile at Del Mar, half-mile at Bakersfield, the Carroll Speedway, and others brought these thoughts to mind: Motorcycle training is good if you want to do car racing because you learn to race handlebar to handlebar, and you get used to having someone close to you!

Today most of your top international competitors have come up from the ranks of kart racing.

Most people who have not raced bikes or karts find that in their first few years of car racing they get nervous having someone racing side by side with them.

Bob's change from two wheels to four came after his late cousin J. C. Lewis, took him to the 1955 Santa Barbara road races. An entirely new world opened up for him. The next year he was to drive his first race at the same circuit:

I watched for about a year before I decided that this was what I was going to

Here I am hot-footing it at age 18 on my Indian 101 Scout. This was 1951, at the old Carroll Speedway in Los Angeles. *Campbell*

do. I bought a Morgan Plus 4 and ran my first race in the Saturday preliminary. I finished third. After the Saturday session, I thought, "Boy, that was great!" There was nothing to it—just go out and play like I did on the street. The great thing was there was no Highway Patrol to watch out for.

Sunday, however, was a different tune. I only placed fourth. I was beaten by a fellow that I beat the day before. I stopped and thought to myself that there was really a lot more to it than just playing around and driving fast. From that point on, I got serious.

I read everything I could find about racing and driving. One of the best books was, and still is, *The Technique of Motor Racing* by Piero Taruffi. It is literally a mathematically calculated book, complete with diagrams and equations that will get nearly any driver through any turn in the world successfully—if the equations are calculated and followed correctly. Although the book was written in the 1950s the concepts remain the same, even with aerodynamic wings and the current extreme downforce. Only the

My first race car in 1955, the #19 Morgan Plus 4. One automobile about which you can't say, "They don't build 'em like they used to." *Marvin Reichler*

speeds in the corners have increased as the tires have such better adhesion and the braking points are now much later, but basically the fastest way around a turn is still the same.

Another book high on my list of important reading is *The Racing Driver: The Theory and Practice of Fast Driving* by Denis Jenkinson. Jenkinson's book is a classic that gives incredible insight into the make-up of a racing driver.

Other US magazines that will help to keep you abreast of the goings-on in motoring are *Automobile, Autoweek, Car and Driver, On Track, Motor Trend, Racer,* and *Road & Track*; but more about these later. Back to racing.

After running the Morgan for a season, I graduated to the modified classes first with a Triumph TR-2 then anything I could get my gloves on. The next couple of years I did everything I could to improve my driving. After studying everything I could find and racing every chance I got (there's no substitute for practice), I really started to get quick, and even more important, smooth and consistent. My thoughts were now, to go faster.

I bought one of the cars used by Kirk Douglas in the movie, *The Racers*, a 2.6 liter Scaglietti-bodied Ferrari. After two races (and two wins) I sold it and bought my first Corvette. That was really the start of my learning how to drive really fast—and boy, did I enjoy it!

For me there was, and still is, no substitute for horsepower. Horsepower is really fun to drive. It can get you out of trouble but just the same it can get you into as much or more if you don't learn to handle it. That 'vette was a good one, and my mechanic, Don Bachtold, was even better. I won the next eighteen out of twenty races and finished second in the other two. That gave me the 1959 West Coast B-Production championship and the Valvoline Corvette Driver of the Year award.

From then on I was driving for other people. I drove a lot of Corvettes, some modified sports cars like Max Balchowsky's *Ol' Yaller* and Frank Arciero's 4.5 liter Ferrari/Maserati, and was well on my way to fame and fortune.

About this time some petty politics entered the racing scene and because I competed in a race put on by one sanctioning body I was banned from the other one. All I wanted to do was race, not play politics. This sort of thing really sickened me. They took away from me a sport that I really loved. So I said, "To hell with racing!" I quit. I got both my helicopter and private pilot license and became a helicopter pilot.

My first *real* race car, at Santa Barbara in 1958. A 2.6 liter Scaglietti-bodied Ferrari that was used in the Kirk Douglas movie, *The Racers*. Look at those skinny tires.

On my way to winning the West Coast B-Production Championship and the Valvoline Corvette Driver of the Year by taking eighteen out of twenty races in 1959. Starting to reap the spoils of victory. *Lester Nehamkin*

I tried for a year, but couldn't get racing out of my mind. It was really in my blood. The bad politics had passed and in 1963, Shelly Washburn approached me to drive one of the new Corvette Sting Rays. I said yes.

Shortly after, Carroll Shelby talked to me about driving his yet-to-be-seen Cobra. At that time he didn't have any money and, worse yet, he still didn't even have a car done. I passed on the deal and stuck with the Corvette. As it turned out, Shelby got some help from Ford and got the Cobra on the track about the same time we brought out the new Corvette. The race was Riverside and the Cobra had Billy Krause at the wheel.

It just flew! It was all we could do to keep up. From that time on, our 'vettes had problems with this new Snake. After one more race, our fellow Corvette driver Dave MacDonald joined Shelby and then so did Ken Miles. My work was really cut out for me, just making the Sting Ray stay with them. Finally, one Sunday at Pomona, I was the quickest. I thought finally we had it all together. But when

we tried to fire the car up for the race the fuel injection packed it in. Fortunately in those days we used street parts and we took a fuel-injection unit off a spectator's car. By the time we got the car together the race was two laps gone but they let me go out anyway. I chased after the pack and as it turned out I was the quickest one out there. I finished in third place.

The next week I got a call from Shelby to drive in place of Ken Miles at the Continental Divide Raceway as Ken had to test a new Cobra and couldn't do the race. I told Carroll I didn't know if I could even drive a Cobra. He responded, "Look here's a ticket. Be on the plane. Do you want to drive the son-of-a-bitch or not?"

I drove it, thinking it was a good opportunity to find out about the competition. Well, as it happened, I won the race and stayed with the team. Then I started beating Corvettes myself.

It wasn't long after that Shelby and Ford Motor Company decided to take an American team to Europe and try to win the World Manufacturers' Championship. Typically the budget was shaved slightly and although the cars and mechanics had been sent from the United States they decided to use American drivers who were already in Europe—Dan Gurney, Masten Gregory, Richie Ginther, and Phil Hill. I made a deal with Shelby that if he paid me what he paid me in the States and covered my expenses I would move to Europe and drive the Cobra. He agreed and I left, two weeks before my first race in Sicily, the Targa Florio.

I thought I'd never learn the circuit in time: it was 44.7 miles long with more than a thousand corners per lap. It was Masten Gregory who was responsible for teaching me how to learn a circuit. He taught me to first do one full lap, looking at everything, then do it by section. I drove over each section of 3–4 kilometers forward and backward, studying the entire circuit for two weeks, eight hours a day, seven days a week. I had every hazard, braking point, and landmark figured out. Fortunately the landmarks I picked were permanent. The Alfa Romeo team painted rocks along the track bright red to designate its various marker points. The night before the race, a practical joker (or competitor) went around the circuit and painted all of the red rocks white like the others.

All of my study paid off. For qualifying you only got one lap because the course was so long. I was the fastest qualifier until Shelby gave Gurney a second lap and he just beat me out. I was teamed with Phil Hill for this race; Phil was astute, a fantastic driver to work with, as well as now a good friend. We were leading our class when suspension failure put us out just past the one-third point.

I stayed with the team for the rest of the Manufacturers' Championship races and we wound up a strong second to Ferrari on our first season's scoreboard in 1964.

The 1964 season's highlight was winning the GT category at the 24 Hours of Le Mans, teamed with Dan Gurney. It was a fantastic feeling and wherever I'd go in Europe after that I was thought of as a Le Mans winner. And not only did we take the GT class but finished a solid fourth place overall in one of the Cobra Daytona Coupes.

It was a wonderful season but it was still a learning season. I would learn a circuit any way I possibly could. At Nürburgring, the Hanseat driving school was in session and so I enrolled. It worked: I became a lot quicker, faster than trying it on my own. At the end of the 1964 season was the first time I really considered myself a true professional. The next step as far as I was concerned was Formula 1.

At the end of the '64 season I got a chance to have my first taste of a Formula 1 car. I was testing the Ford GT 40 at Monza for John Wyer, and was invited by Alf Francis, Stirling Moss' former mechanic, to test the ATS. I wanted to, but John said not until I had finished testing the GT 40. I finished the five days of GT 40 testing and couldn't wait for the next day's adventure. Formula 1 in those days was far less structured and much less professional. They didn't even use seat belts yet.

When I took the ATS out for the first time it felt a little uncomfortable. It was set up for Mario Cabrall, a 5ft, 4in Portuguese Grand Prix driver. My head stuck out above the rollbar and there were no seat belts! After an hour of testing I felt comfortable and confident. It was great!

Now all I needed was some thinking time.

At dinner that night we were discussing who we figured had gotten through the famous Curva Grande flat out and we figured only about six F1 drivers had done it at that time. It was about a 150mph turn. Well, for the session in the morning I had resolved to myself that I was going to give it a try. It took about eight laps before I did it and when I did I had a rush that was about like swallowing my heart. I held my breath all of the way around the turn. At the exit I glanced at the tach and I had come out of the turn about 300rpm faster. I couldn't do it every lap—only once every seven or eight to start with—then I got so I could do it flat out about every three or four. I just couldn't do it every lap. It was scary! Finally I got my last "in" sign and the session was over. I thought to myself that I didn't know when I'd be in a Formula 1 car again at Monza so I'd try the Curva

"The essence of high-performance driving, be it on the street or on the racetrack, is to control weight transfer in order to maximize traction during the basic functions of braking, cornering, and acceleration."

One of the great thrills of my life—winning the GT category at Le Mans in 1964 with Dan Gurney. *Bernard Cahier*

Grande just one more time flat out at about 150mph.

There's a large ancient tree on the right-hand side of the turn and its roots run under the track, causing a bump right in the racing line of the pavement. I entered that infamous turn as usual. I hit the bump as usual, but this time the left rear halfshaft broke, the wheel flew off, and the car swung violently to the left. I tried to spin the car back and forth to scrub off the speed. But there was only one rear wheel working and only one front wheel steering—the right one was totally off the ground because the left rear was gone. There was no way could I save it.

I was just along for the ride: the car took control and shot through the hedge that lined the curve (no Armco rails then), backward then into a ravine. I got catapulted out of the car, straight through a tree. I was wearing a plastic-bubble face shield and it was shredded off my helmet. I landed flat on my back on a huge pile of leaves. I thought I was dead. I remember flying through the hedge thinking to myself, "Shit, Bondurant, you just wrote yourself off."

That was the last thing I remembered before waking up on my back. When I came to I was gasping for breath. I thought that I'd punctured a lung and broken every bone in my body. My mind flashed back to the crash, and knowing I had been flat out in sixth it had to be a horrific crash. Without trying to get up, and still gasping for breath, I tried to move things. First my toes, feet, fingers, hands, legs, and arms.

Somehow it all worked and it was still all there. I couldn't believe it. The impact had just knocked the wind out of me. I rolled over on my stomach, got up

on my hands and knees, and started looking for the car. I couldn't find it. I thought to myself, "I know I came down here in a car. Where is it?" I crawled back through the hedge, still on my hands and knees. Finally I was able to stand and found the car. When I found it, I realized just how lucky I really was. The real luck, in this case, was that I was not wearing a seat belt. After I was thrown out of the cockpit, the car went through a tree, taking off the windshield, the top of the steering wheel, the top of the seat, the top of the rollbar, and even the top of the engine. If I would have stayed with the car I would have been decapitated.

With that experience behind me I really had some long and serious thoughts. Did I really want to race Formula 1? Fortunately the only injury I sustained was a slight back injury that was taken care of in England after five days of heat treatments, rubdowns, and adjustments.

From England, I had come directly to the States to drive one of Shelby's rear-engined King Cobras in the West Coast Fall races. I really wanted to drive it a lot and didn't tell anybody about my ATS crash at Monza.

Riverside was the first race and we had tire testing for Goodyear for the five days before the race. Every day, on the way to the circuit, I would stop and get my back worked on by a chiropractor before testing. Finally by race day I was feeling better.

Everything was looking fine. This was just the Saturday preliminary but a good finish meant a good starting position for the Sunday main event. Unfortunately, it wasn't noticed until the end of the first lap but Jim Hall's Chaparral had dropped automatic transmission fluid all over the starting line. Normally an oil flag is displayed some distance before the spill but this time it was right over it.

The start went well—Bruce McLaren was leading, Dan Gurney was second, I was third, and Walt Hansgen was right behind me—running so close that I didn't see the oil or the flag. I just touched the oil with my right-side tire, started to lose it, just about got it saved, and Walt tapped my left rear. Away it went! Here I was doing 120mph plus, backward, heading for the Turn One guardrail. Looking over my shoulder I was thinking, "Holy shit! That guardrail's going to shove that engine right through my back!" I pulled a quick reverse 180degree spin in the other direction and tore the nose off the car instead, but it didn't hurt my back. The race was red-flagged with both the oil and my car spread all over the first corner.

In those days, for the main event of the weekend, there was a catch-all race on Sunday morning for the final few qualifying positions to give the give the top nonfinishers of the Saturday heat race a chance to make the final grid. My car was put back together overnight and so was Dan Gurney's and Bobby Unser's, who also didn't finish the heat race. We ran the catch-all with quite a few others. Dan won, I was second, and Bobby third. This gave us forty-first, forty second, and forty-third positions on the grid.

For the main event, as they rolled my car into position, I asked my mechanic if they had changed my brake pads after the qualifying race. No? They forgot! Not enough time now, maybe they'll last two-thirds the distance. They lasted just slightly longer, then it was metal-to-metal, and that didn't slow me down well. With luck I ended up fifth and at the next race at Laguna Seca a good solid third. That season with the King Cobras was a wild time—I really enjoyed it all. They were fantastic.

In 1965, I went back to Europe and drove the Cobras most of the time. At Le Mans I drove the Ford GT 40 with a

My handlebar-to-handlebar motorcycle racing was excellent experience for times like this: the Monterey Grand Prix in 1964. I have got Roger Penske right in front of me, Dan Gurney immediately next door and Ed Leslie, Parnelli Jones, Don Wester, Ronnie Buckman, Bruce McLaren, and a whole bunch of other guys right on my tail. *Dave Friedman*

351ci engine. I was happy as I was third-fastest qualifier. Chris Amon was fastest in a new Ford Mark 2 with a 427 engine, then John Surtees in a Ferrari, then myself ahead of Bruce McLaren in a second 427 Ford Mk 2. Behind Bruce were some more Ferraris and then the rest of the Ford GT 40s.

That could have been a great race but unfortunately Ford made some special "super-duper" racing cylinder heads and had them sent especially for the race. It turned out they were for the wrong engine block and the water jackets didn't quite line up and we were all out of the race after the first two-and-a-half or three hours. It was a shame.

The GT 40 was an incredible car. I remember going down the Mulsanne straight in qualifying at 212mph. I got so I could do the kink near the end of the straight without lifting, then brake hard for the 45mph Mulsanne corner. Incredible! That car worked so super it was unbelievable. A fantastic car to drive!

The year 1965 was a fantastic one for Bob. He drove Formula 3 for Ken Tyrrell, where he set the fastest lap at Monaco (a new Formula 3 record at the time) and

drove the Cobras in the World Manufacturers' Championship. Bob co-drove to win the coveted GT class title in eight out of ten races to give a happy Carroll Shelby and Ford the much sought after World Manufacturers' Championship title over the factory Ferrari team. This championship gave the United States its first World Championship title.

All that was left for Bob now was another shot at Formula 1. That wasn't far off. Ferrari gave Bob a contract to drive its sports cars in the Manufacturers' Championship races for the following year and a works Formula 1 drive for the 1965 US Grand Prix at Watkins Glen in October:

Not a bad team for my first Formula 1 race. The best part about it was the team and the car. The worst thing about the race was the weather—it was horrible. Rain. Most of the race I ran about sixth, while doing so I couldn't help thinking, "Not too bad." But it got worse.

The heavy rain stretched the elastic band on my goggles (they didn't make full-face helmets then) and they kept falling down. If they had been new they would have been OK but they were old and so were the extra pair I had in my pit

An unbelievable car, the Ford GT 40. Here I am at the Mulsanne Corner after qualifying third fastest at Le Mans in 1965. I took it down the Mulsanne Straight at 212mph—wow!

so it wouldn't help to stop and change them. I kept on with one hand holding the goggles in place and the other driving. When shifting or in a corner I would put my face into the wind to help hold them on. Not a good end to my first Formula 1 race. I finished up ninth in a race that I should have done much better in had it not been for an old but necessary piece of equipment that I took for granted.

Driving sports cars for Ferrari was rewarding but it was the other things that happened in 1966 that really made it a year to look back on with good memories. Formula 1 was to be the direction for my season. Everything fell into place.

In 1964, I had done some driving instruction at Carroll Shelby's racing school and in '65 after the season was over, I was at Riverside testing. John Timanus, who was then instructing at Shelby's school told me that John Frankenheimer was looking for some people to drive in a film that he was going to do about Grand Prix racing. Frankenheimer and I met and he asked me if I would like to drive in his film. I replied, "Sure, but not if it's going to be some Mickey Mouse racing film." He exploded! "It's going to be the best damn film you ever saw!"

I was testing the new GT350 Shelby Mustangs a couple of days later at Willow Springs, and Frankenheimer came along. He asked me all sorts of different questions about what I'd do if this happened or that happened and one of the questions was what would I do if I went off the road. The first thing, I told him, was to turn the wheel straight so that a wheel wouldn't dig in the dirt and roll the car. All through the day while riding with me he kept asking all sorts of questions.

Nearing the end of the day I was moving along about 110 or 115 coming

I'm at the wheel of the Daytona Cobra #26, about to lap one of my teammates. This was Reims and it was here that we clinched the 1965 World Manufacturers' Championship on July 4th, finally beating the Ferrari deadlock. *Geoffrey Goddard*

Formula 1, at last. My first F1 race and for Ferrari, too! This was taken in practice at "the Glen" in upstate New York before my goggles started to slip.

through Turn Nine. The Santa Ana winds were blowing sand across the track and the car's drift angle was increasing. I realized we weren't going to make it through the turn. I was busy driving the car off the road, turning the wheel straight, charging through the sage brush and sand, and I hadn't given Frankenheimer a second thought. Finally we slowed to a stop. I asked him if he was OK. He didn't say a word for a few seconds. "You alright, John?" I asked. He yells, "That was fantastic! You did exactly what you said you'd do. That's really fantastic." I asked him if he wanted to get out and watch but no, he kept riding with me. I really respect him for that.

It wasn't until almost a year later, at the end of filming the movie *Grand Prix*, that I told him that my going off the road wasn't on purpose.

Despite—or perhaps because of—going off the road, Frankenheimer hired me as a technical consultant for his film *Grand Prix*. I did a little bit of everything: I drove camera cars as well as the race cars in the racing scenes. It was great. I drove just about every day in a single-seater. As I look back on it now, probably the best thing that I did was to teach the actors in the film how to drive. Not just the stars but also John Stevens, the director of photography, and the film editor too. I taught James Garner, Yves Montand, Brian Bedford, and Antonio Sabato. Little did I know it then, but this teaching was just a start.

Because of working in the film, I was able to drive every Grand Prix circuit for about two weeks before every Formula 1 race and again for about two weeks after it. All this worked well for me because by the first race of the 1966 season I had a Formula 1 drive.

The year 1966 was one of change in Formula 1, moving from 1.5 liter to 3.0

liter engines in one big jump. This meant all the cars had to be new and the engines were sure not to be fully developed until mid-season. While awaiting the 3.0 liter engines, many of the teams were forced to use existing 2.0 liter engines in the interim.

I drove for a private entrant, Bernard White. His team was one of those with the 2.0 liter cars. Bernard had a 2.0 liter BRM that was built for the Tasman Series as a spare car for Jackie Stewart and Graham Hill on the works BRM team. We also used the car for filming in the movie *Grand Prix*. Formula 1 was great even if I wasn't in a "factory car." I learned a lot and really loved racing in Europe.

In the early part of the season my car was quite competitive with the factory teams but, as anticipated, by mid-season the works teams started getting it right and we were quickly left behind. The first race was at Monaco, one of my favorite circuits, and also turned out to be the best finish of my Formula 1 career. I managed a fourth place behind Jackie Stewart in a BRM, Lorenzo Bandini in a Ferrari, and Graham Hill in the second factory BRM. I really felt great, I was racing for the Drivers' World Championship. But that turned out to be the season's highpoint. The team was on a minimal budget, the preparation of the car was nearly nonexistent, and finally at Monza, I quit.

At the US Grand Prix at Watkins Glen I drove for Dan Gurney in his four-cylinder Eagle and wound up the season driving his V-12 Eagle at the Mexico City Grand Prix.

With no hot prospects for a first-rate Formula 1 ride in the 1967 season I decided to stay in the United States and see what was available rather than take another shot at a poorly prepared "also-ran" Formula 1 team.

There was in the United States, a lot of interest in the United States Road Racing Championship (USRRC) and the Can-Am series (Canadian-American Challenge Series). Each of these series used the same cars: Group 7 sports racers with big engines and lots of horsepower. This caught my interest.

Some of the driving crew from *Grand Prix*. Left to right are: Graham Hill, Jochen Rindt, James Garner, Guy Liger, Dan Gurney, Jo Schlesser, Bruce McLaren, Antonio Sabato, and Jo Siffert.

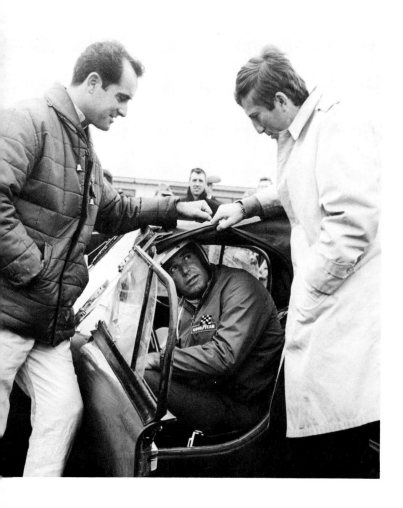

James Garner, my "star" pupil for the movie *Grand Prix*, was a tight fit in a 289 Cobra. The late World Champion, Jochen Rindt, and I give him some pointers before he did a hot lap at Watkins Glen.

Peter Revson liked the looks of the series too and we teamed together for the Dana Chevrolet team. Peyton Cramer ran the team and we were to get new Lola T-70s (that was the hot number to have) but we wound up with McLaren MkIIs and they were dogs. Not at all competitive or reliable compared with the Lolas or Chaparrals.

Peter and I drove hard at the Riverside opener and only placed third and fourth. And that was our best race of the season. It seemed like some little thing or another was forever plaguing us.

That's what happened at Watkins Glen. Only it wasn't something little—it was a big one! I was traveling at about 150mph, coming out of a corner onto the top straight, when a steering arm broke. The McLaren steered itself and rocketed straight toward a dirt embankment. I could see a bad one coming! It's funny what you think about in a split second. First, I shut down the fuel pumps so I wouldn't burn. Then I shut off the engine (I didn't want to blow it up). Until the crash is all over it doesn't really feel like you are going to be hurt. It's kind of like watching TV; you're just a spectator and it seems like it's happening around you but not really to you.

Since the steering didn't respond any-

At the wheel of the 2.0 liter BRM at Brands Hatch during my 1966 Formula 1 season. *Bernard Cahier*

more, just prior to my inevitable impact, I released my grip on the wheel so I wouldn't break my thumbs, wrists, or arms. I took a deep breath and tried to relax. I was going straight into the dirt embankment! When I hit the dirt bank the car was launched in the air and as it started to fly, the impact peeled the aluminum floorpan back clear to the rear bulkhead. These McLarens had complete monocoque chassis and didn't have any cross tubes in the cockpit so my feet fell out the bottom. The car rolled end over end and then snap-rolled sideways eight times before coming to a stop. Every time it rolled my dangling feet and legs were smashed. But I was really fortunate. As violent as the crash was I only ended up with a shattered right heel, two broken ankles, some broken ribs, a chip out of a vertebra, and a chunk out of my forehead. The good news was that I was alive and could be repaired.

But then the bad news: I was instantly out of the racing business and in the hospital.

The second day I was in the hospital I got a yellow-lined notepad and a pen and started to plan something that I had been thinking about for a long time. Since helping out Shelby in his racing school and after training the actors and crew for the movie *Grand Prix*, I had been thinking that someday I'd like to have a driving school. I planned it on paper: a high-performance driving school.

While in Europe I tried some different schools and worked with Jim Russell in order to use his facilities to train the people in *Grand Prix*. This looked like the right time to give this a try. The first experiences I had training people at Shelby's were fantastic. I really loved it. It's a super feeling that you get watching them get better and quicker from what you have taught them. James Garner was a perfect example. For the movie *Grand Prix*, he did a fantastic job driving real Formula 1 cars. I started him out at Willow Springs Raceway in a Shelby GT350 Mustang then put him in a 289 Cobra, then a Lotus Formula Ford, then finally into a Lotus Tasman Formula 1 car. He did fantastic!

Many of these thoughts crossed my mind while I was laying in that hospital bed, so I worked out a plan of how to put it all together and start a school.

As I got closer and closer to being well, my mind was more intent on going racing again and the school idea took a back seat. I formed a company with Don Rabbitt, a former Shelby PR man; Dick Guldstrand, Corvette driver and ace mechanic; and Sandy Sandine, a fine engineer. We called it American International Racing Corporation and we set our sights on building a turbine car to run the FIA endurance races at Daytona, Sebring, and Le Mans. We were all set to go, sponsors and all, when the FIA changed the rules from an unlimited displacement to a 3.0 liter-engine displacement, which would have made the turbine car non-competitive. We got two Corvettes, but the other partners were each wanting something other than the original agreement so I resigned. The time had come to start my driving school. I pulled out my hospital notes and went on from there.

Out of necessity, the step-by-step program that I put together in the hospital called for everything to be sponsored with the exception of the rent. That was the only way I would be able to start. I organized my driving school like I would a race team, and with the sponsors, I was able to have the best equipment. I put together presentations for all my potential sponsors and I got most of the ones I wanted to participate.

I reached a deal with Datsun and opened my first school on Valentine Day, February 14, 1968, at the Orange County Raceway near Los Angeles. Not too many cars then—a Volkswagen camper, a new Datsun 510 sedan, two new Datsun 2000 roadsters, a Formula Vee, and my Lola camera car. I stayed at Orange County for two-and-a-half years until the new Ontario Motor Speedway opened nearby.

When I first moved to Ontario, I also switched from Datsun to Porsche for my school cars and replaced the Formula Vee cars with Formula Fords. As time passed, Datsun introduced the new Z cars and we were reunited.

Ontario was a beautiful facility but it was always burdened financially and its burdens eventually became mine too, as my rent soared way out of reach. It was either close down or move. Some choice. So, I moved to Sears Point International Raceway in the Sonoma wine country,

This is the McLaren MkII that helped me get into the driving school business after it nearly killed me.

not far from San Francisco. When I made the move Datsun stayed with me.

My fleet continued to expand and year by year it was upgraded. In 1982, the Datsuns gave way to the latest Ford Mustang GTs and Crossle Formula Fords. I now use 5.0 liter V-8, five-speed Ford Mustang GTs with specially modified suspension; Ford Thunderbird Turbo Coupes (with 5.0 liter V-8, five-speed transmissions, and limited-slip differentials); Ford Taurus SHO and Mercury Sables with SHO running gear as well as new Crossle Formula Fords. All of my fleet are specially prepared and modified, including all of the necessary safety equipment for high-performance driving and proper instruction. My Ford Mustangs are clearly the fastest cars we've used for my school short of the Ford GT 40. The Crossle For-

Motorcycle training is good if you want to do car racing because you learn to race handlebar to handlebar, and you get used to having someone close to you!

My current fleet of instruction cars at my new home, Firebird International Raceway in Phoenix, Arizona.

On my feet again after my Watkins Glen accident, proudly displaying my first fleet of instruction vehicles.

23

One of my earliest jobs with the school was technical advisor and camera car driver for the movie *Winning*. Here I am at Indy driving my Lola T-70 camera car, which we designed and built especially for the film.

mula Fords really fill the bill as great open-wheel racers.

In 1991, I decided to move the school to Firebird Raceway in Phoenix, Arizona. Sears Point is really a fantastic circuit, but my school simply was getting too big for our limited space.

Besides having a lot more facility space at Firebird, I was able to design my own circuit specially for teaching. We now have more than five track variations on permanent circuits as well as large areas set aside for handling ovals, skid con-

trol, autocross, and accident avoidance. Our safety facilities at this track are of the highest standards. Because of the size and design of the circuits, we have lots of run-off area on most corners as well as energy-absorbing sand pits in critical turns. Our students can concentrate on driving and learning, not on worrying about what will happen if you get a wheel off course.

The Bob Bondurant School of High Performance Driving has become the

Two of the first Bondurant school graduates, Robert Wagner and Paul Newman. I trained them to drive for the movie *Winning*.

standard by which all others are evaluated. After more than twenty-five years, the Bondurant school has become a school that is unparalleled in the world of driving instruction. Bob's school is highly respected and officially recognized both domestically and internationally in the motorsports community. The driving programs that Bob offers are of increasingly greater variety. There is something there for everyone, from his teenage driving programs to his advanced classes for vintage racers. There is a lot in between, too.

The standard bill of fare is a one day advanced street driving course that includes skid control and accident avoidance, a two- or three-day high-performance driving class, and a four-day grand prix competition road-racing class that will teach you how to drive Ford Mustang GTs and Formula Fords.

In addition to the programmed classes Bob offers special one-on-one instruction for the advanced driver as well as the advanced racer. Most of the NASCAR drivers, as well as many other professional drivers, come to Bob's school to refine and improve their skills. Bob's advanced instruction really dials the driver in to just what he or she as well as the car is capable of doing. The instruction can be in either one of the school cars or the student's own car.

In recent years, Bob has added the Bondurant Law Enforcement academy for police and sheriffs and one he calls his Executive Protection course, which teaches drivers and chauffeurs how to get away from potential kidnappers and assassins. He has designed many group courses (from five or ten people up to 150) for major corporations that promote incentive and help bond the employees into a close knit team. He also offers a stunt driving course and puts together many special programs designed for motion picture production as well as courses for any specialty driving talent needed.

No matter how specialized the area of training that is required, the Bob Bondurant School of High Performance Driving has or will make the facilities available for nearly any form of driving instruction.

Since the opening of Bob's school, racing has perhaps taken a back seat to in-

As I said before, I like driving lots of horsepower and Dick Barbour's Twin Turbo 935 Porsche really moved. This was Sears Point in 1979.

Typical of my Executive Protection and Law Enforcement Academy programs, all of our students get hands-on, behind-the-wheel experience.

struction but Bob is by no means retired. He keeps his helmet and gloves ready to take to the wheel in competition anytime he has the opportunity. By the time he opened his original school Bob was ready for racing again and jumped right back into Can-Am, Formula 5000, endurance racing, IMSA-prepared 935 Turbo Porsches, sprint cars, and Grand National stock cars—and still continues in historic and vintage racing. There is no end in sight to Bob's racing career. He is just as sharp and competitive as he always was. He still does many hours at speed each

Among the wide variety of cars I've enjoyed driving was this quarter-mile dirt track sprint car. I'm just hot lapping to see what it's like. It's great!
John Monhoff

week, testing and developing new school cars and courses, and keeping his instructors on their toes. He still has a trick or two to teach them, even those who have been with him for many years. His feelings are clear when he speaks of racing:

I still do race from time to time for several reasons. First and foremost, I love to race. It's fun, exciting, challenging, and keeps the adrenaline flowing. For me the only thing that comes close to it is sex.

From a more practical view, I also race to keep abreast of what is going on with contemporary cars. I try to race current cars that are competitive in their classes so that I can work that into my training programs. Many of my teaching staff, most of whom have been with me for many years, race presently and in a wide variety of cars—everything from SCCA club racing to full-blown Interna-

tional competition. I encourage their racing and do what I can to support their careers. Not only are my instructors good competitors but more important to the learning process, they are excellent instructors and can communicate what they have to teach their students in a highly professional fashion.

Although there is no substitute for actual behind-the-wheel training, proper driving technique is also arrived at through instruction, thinking, and practice. The goal of this book is to give the reader the insight and instruction to come to terms with his or her self as well as with the car. Although reading and studying is just the first step to actualizing technique, this study helps to form the basics. Practice and utilization will in fact make you a better driver but it is important to make use of the basics and proven methods to ar-

I was the fastest qualifier and set a new lap record in this 1980 Buick at Sears Point. I wound up second at the checkered flag in this NASCAR race.

rive at your full high-performance driving potential.

A high-performance driver is one who drives, not only to the fullest capabilities of the car, but also to the fullest capabilities of oneself.

One of my best "students"—Gypsy Bondurant. *Bob Jordan*

2

Getting to Know the Terms

The following pages introduce you to the world of high-performance driving. By picking up this book you have taken the first steps to improving your driving ability and, at the same time, your driving pleasure.

Before we get into the hows and whys, it is important to briefly define a few terms that are used regularly throughout the text. To many, these words are already familiar but to others they may create some confusion as to what they really mean.

Each term will be dealt with in a later chapter of the book but here is a starter of brief explanations to get you going. All of these terms relate to cornering and/or traction.

Oversteer: Rear Wheel Skid or Slide

When you have adhesion and traction with the front wheels of the car, but the rear wheels lose traction and slide towards the outside of the corner. The oversteer can be to either left or right and its effect decreases the radius of the turn.

Oversteer is also referred to as being "loose" or "coming around on you."

Understeer: Front Wheel Skid or Slide

When you have adhesion and traction with the rear wheels of the car but the front wheels lose traction and, regardless of the steering correction, the front of the car slides to the outside of the corner. Understeer increases the radius of the corner.

Understeer is also referred to as "pushing" or "plowing."

Throttle Steer

Throttle steer refers to the amount of throttle applied in a corner. The amount of throttle steer can induce oversteer or understeer with all configurations of engine and final-drive layouts. Proper throttle steer is a balance of gas and traction regulated by the driver. The amount of throttle applied will dictate the amount of steering that must be dialed in. There must be a balance of throttle and steering to maximize traction.

Line

Line refers to the physical lines of movement that a car takes through any given corner from entry, to apex area, to exit. A line can be either good or bad, right or wrong.

Apex Area

The apex of a corner is the *area of a corner* where the car is in its most stable position, not just a clipping point, where the inside front wheel runs closest to the inside of a given corner.

An example of a controlled powerslide, oversteering in one of my school Formula Fords in a right-hand corner.

Here I am leading the late Pedro Rodriquez at Riverside. Pedro's Ferrari is very "loose"—a good example of oversteer. *Dave Friedman*

Where the apex area is in a corner directly relates to how the corner is entered and will definitely effect how and where it is exited. An apex area varies in length and location from corner to corner. It can be early or late, long or short.

Trail-Brake

After the major braking for a corner has been completed, trail braking is, essentially, just riding the brake into the first third of the corner, gradually releasing the pressure and smoothly switching from

See how the front wheels of the Formula Ford are pushing to the outside of the corner in this example of understeer. The car is not going where the front wheels are pointing.

A good example of low-speed understeer. This is me in the Gurney Eagle Weslake V-12 Formula 1 car in the hairpin, looking where I want to go, at the Mexico City Grand Prix in 1966. *David Phipps*

For me there was, and still is, no substitute for horsepower. Horsepower is really fun to drive. It can get you out of trouble but just the same it can get you into as much or more if you don't learn to handle it.

brake to throttle.

By trail-braking you maintain chassis set. The front shocks and springs are compressed and you maintain a froward-directed weight transfer creating more downforce on the front wheels. This increases the tire contact patches, which maximizes traction and provides better control.

Tire Contact Patch

A tire contact patch is the area on the bottom of the tire that is in direct contact with the road. The tire contact patch can vary in size and shape with the tire type, size, kind of car, the attitude of the car on the road, the suspension, and also whether entering or exiting a corner. De-

Just like a train, notice how all five Can-Am cars are following me through pretty much the same line, down the Corkscrew at Laguna Seca in 1970.

The late Mike Parkes is right behind my Tim Parnell Team Brabham on the proper line in the apex area of this corner at the Reims Circuit in France. I seem to be a little too wide...it was my first Formula 2 race.

Just as in downhill ski racing, being airborne looks impressive, but in order to corner, brake, and go fast you want maximum contact with the road surface. I was driving this factory Porsche Carrera at the Nürburgring in Germany, 1966. Being airborne is just part of going fast here.

pending on the transfer of weight of a car, acceleration, braking, or turning, one tire can have a different tire contact patch than the other three. Tire contact patch varies constantly.

Ideally one wants the maximum tire contact patch possible in contact with the road. Trail-braking helps to control the tire contact patches of all four tires while entering a turn just as smooth acceleration helps steer while coming out of a corner.

Drifting

Drifting is, or should be, a controlled function. It is directly opposed to sliding or skidding, which are out-of-control conditions.

Drifting is a balance. The rear of the car can drift with throttle control as can the front. The optimum condition one wants to create is an evenness that permits the entire car, front and rear, to drift in a balanced lateral motion on the border of maximum traction. This drifting effect utilizes gravity forces (inertia forces) on all aspects of the car, allowing it to travel its fastest at a speed just past the absolute limit of maximum adhesion.

A typical Corvette four-wheel drift. This was in 1960—it's the same today only at faster speeds. Look how skinny the tires were then! *George Robitschek*

Weight Transfer

Weight transfer is the forward, back, or lateral movement of the loaded weight of a car under acceleration, braking, and cornering. The static weight of the car transfers forward, rearward, or side to side during the time a car is in motion.

A stopped car has a determined weight balance or bias. A moving car, because of suspension and movement, finds that weight balance or bias constantly shifting. For example, the moving weight of the car transfers forward under braking. Under acceleration the weight transfers to the rear. During cornering the moving weight transfers laterally. Simply put, the sprung weight of the car transfers to different areas of the car during movement.

The second day I was in the hospital I got a yellow-lined notepad and a pen and started to plan something that I had been thinking about for a long time. I planned it on paper: a high-performance driving school.

Here's Al Unser, Jr., at 19, practicing what I taught him. It takes a lot of practice to avoid being out of control in a slide or skid. Just about to the point of no return on our skid pad, but he caught this one.

3

Getting the Right Fit

One of the most important and yet most overlooked basics in driving any car is, clearly and simply, comfort. If you aren't comfortable in the car you just won't drive it as well, nor will you enjoy driving it as much either.

When I say comfortable I don't mean driving from an over-stuffed easy-chair. That deadens sensitivity; I want you to *maximize sensitivity*. It is of utmost importance to sit properly so that you can easily operate all of the controls and so your body can *feel* what the car is doing under it.

Optimizing Seating Position and Posture

The essence of high-performance driving, be it on the street or on the race-track, is to control weight transfer in order to maximize traction during the basic functions of braking, cornering, and acceleration. To have that control you must be seated properly. Tilt the back of your seat to a more upright position. When you're

sitting upright, your mind is sharper and you think and react quicker!

All of your sources of input give you your ability to control your car but the two major things that affect your performance are *what you see* and *what your body feels*. Everything that the car does is transmitted right back to you through the seat, steering wheel, and foot pedals. The ideal driving position is one that allows your body to maximize the input that is available to it. This input comes from your whole body, your legs and buttocks, from the base of your spine, up your back, hands, arms, neck, eyes, all feeding information to your brain telling you what you need to do. The optimum seating position is one that has as much of your body as possible in contact with your seat.

You should have your buttocks tucked well into the crotch of the seat so you can feel what the car is doing with your fanny, the back of your legs, and your lower and upper back. You should be sitting as up-right as possible because it helps to make you more alert.

The proper seating position. Arms bent, seated upright with fanny tucked into the crotch of the seat. Legs should be slightly bent, too. Shoulder harness is snug.

The infamous Bondurant van ride—one of the most memorable tours around a racetrack circuit one will ever experience.

When driving a formula racing car or sports racer it is a lot more difficult to sit upright—they are designed almost strictly for aerodynamics and the seating is dictated by the design. When fitting those kind of seats, if you pad the middle to upper part of the seats to sit as upright as possible, your mind will be sharper and you can react quicker. A production racer or street car is designed with a different purpose in mind and it is possible to modify the car so that you are able to sit upright, in the best position possible.

Dan Gurney was the one who taught me the importance of a proper seating position. I remember, in the 1950s, when we were both racing Corvettes. Dan was sitting "bolt-upright." He never moved. He was like a statue sitting in the driver's seat. He taught me, I listened, and he was right.

Sitting upright is where it all begins. The seats of modern production cars are much better fit than the old bench-type seat of yesterday but even so, you might want to replace your stock seat with a unit such as a Recaro adjustable one that has lumbar support. With a Recaro, you'll really get a better car feel, you will experience less fatigue, and it's a lot more comfortable.

Your seat should be adjusted so that you have a bent-arm driving position and the controls fall into easy reach. Distance from the seat to the steering wheel is really important and the extremes should be avoided. The first World Champion, Giuseppe Farina, drove in the straight-arm style. He sat so far back from the wheel that his arms were unbent and most of the steering had to be done with his shoulders. It is not only a fatiguing way to drive but also much less precise. The tires were at that time much narrower and the grip was poor so it really didn't require as much strength to steer then as it does now. Today's cars steer harder due to the extra-wide tires, so it takes more physical strength, especially with the smaller steering wheels, like in formula cars.

The other extreme would be Richard Petty driving NASCAR Winston Cup stock cars. Richard practically sits right on the steering wheel. For the NASCAR ovals it's all right but if you have to react quickly in a street or road-racing situation you won't have enough room to move freely.

Here's that nice McLaren that exhausted me at Mosport, Canada. I can't emphasize too much the importance of good comfort and proper seating to help you drive up to your car's maximum potential.

Note the extra padding we've placed on the seat to provide a better fit for singer, song writer, and actor Paul Williams, one of my most loyal students.

One of the most important and yet most overlooked basics in driving any car is, clearly and simply, *comfort*. If you aren't comfortable in the car you just won't drive it as well, nor will you enjoy driving it as much either.

The best position is somewhere between the two. For your distance gauge, you should be able to rest the bend in your wrist just at the top of the steering wheel when you are at rest. While driving, you want your hands about at the 3:00 and 9:00 position on the wheel, with your elbows bent at an angle of about 120 to 140 degrees. In a street car if your seating position is poor then you will become more easily fatigued, less alert, and more likely to fall asleep at the wheel on a long trip. In a racing car, you simply won't be as fast, consistent, or smooth. Combine that with early fatigue and you just won't do too well.

In 1971, at the start of the Can-Am season, I was driving for the Paul Newman-sponsored team with Lothar Motschenbacher. We had brand new McLarens (that was the right car to have that season). Lothar's car was the first delivered and it was all completed and race-ready before mine had even arrived.

When mine finally came, it was loaded on the transporter and was literally put together on the way to the first race, at Mosport. It was worked on all the way, in the back of the transporter and was finally finished up at the track. My dialing-in time was cut to just a few laps. I had twenty minutes in the car to do a shakedown, qualify, feel what the car was doing, and figure out what the suspension and brake bias changes had to be. I got the car sorted, but what I didn't realize was that we hadn't padded the seat at all. I was so intent on getting the car sorted out right and qualifying that I completely overlooked the seating compartment.

As it was, the car sorted well. Lothar and I turned identical times and took third and fourth fastest on the grid. Even at the start of the race I still didn't realize that we hadn't adjusted my seat (the only way the seat of a Can-Am car was adjusted was by adding padding). About a third of the way through the race I was starting to get tired—I was in great shape then and used to endurance driving. The problem was, I was sitting too far back from the steering wheel and my arms were fully extended to steer the car through the corners. So, I was steering with my wrists and my shoulders instead of my forearms and biceps, as I would have in a normal bent-arm position, where I had more power and strength. So, as my arms got more tired, I would pull myself forward in the seat with the steering wheel, up to a bent-arm position, drive five or six laps flat out, then I'd relax my arms for a few laps, and then do the sequence again.

At the end of the race I was exhausted. I finished fourth but I know that if my seating position had been normal I would have been able to finish second or third at least, because the car was working great.

Seat Belts, Shoulder Harnesses, and Submarine Belts

To maximize the way your body fits

One way to counteract cornering forces is by tilting your head into the corner—but keep as much of you as possible in contact with the seat. This is the Freiburg, Germany hill climb, where I took first place with the Cobra in 1964.

the seat, and have it make proper contact, you must also take into consideration your seat belt, shoulder harness, and submarine belt or crawl strap.

In racing, the importance of tight seat belts can't be stressed too much. If your belt or harness is at all loose, the forces of cornering and braking will cause you to slide in the seat, causing you to have to concentrate on bracing yourself with your arms, feet, or body. This is not only detracting from your driving concentration but is also fatiguing. This also applies to street driving.

Seat belts must be worn at all times, street or track. They are cheap life insurance and help hold you in place, allowing you to feel just what your car is doing at all times.

Make sure the seat belts are snug. Sliding around in the seat is distracting and doesn't let you read the input coming from the car correctly. Another simple reason for strapping the belts tight is that most nylon belts stretch. If you happen to roll the car and your belt is not tight enough you'll probably hit your head on the roof—or worse if it's an open car.

Shoulder harnesses also help drivers avoid leaning their bodies into the turns. Remember Dan Gurney in the Corvette, "Like a statue!" If you have to lean into a turn then you are reducing the contact area of your back and body to the seat, thereby reducing the input area for the car to tell you what is going on. Leaning also increases your fatigue rate and slightly alters your visual perspective. If you feel that you have to lean to offset the g forces because your car corners so well—or perhaps your suspension is so soft you can't see out of the window if you don't lean—then try just tilting your head, not your whole upper body.

If you have an open car and are concerned about being strapped in during a rollover, then install a rollbar. Racing cars, open or closed, have rollover protection

The 3:00 and 9:00 position. Notice the way my thumbs rest on the short padded sections of this road car's steering wheel.

as a mandatory rule for safety, even in Showroom Stock classes. If you think that you might need it with your driving technique on the street then don't take any chances. Put one in. Open car or closed car, safe is sane. Rollbars also tend to stiffen the chassis of a car, making it handle better, thus sending more input right up the driver's seat.

My hands at the 3:00 and 9:00 position on a Formula race car steering wheel.

Now make a turn keeping your hands in the same location on the steering wheel.

Everything that the car does is transmitted right back to you through the seat, steering wheel, and foot pedals. The ideal driving position is one that allows your body to maximize the input that is available to it.

Steering Wheel Grip

Now that you know how to sit in your car, it's time to get you hands on something meaningful...the steering wheel.

The kind, size, and shape of the steering wheel is up to you but don't get a rim so thick or so thin that it is difficult to get a good grip on it. The size and thickness of the wheel are important for *car feel*.

I like the leather-covered wheel that has padding coming down onto the spokes so I can put my thumbs on top comfortably. On the Cobras I used to tape sponge rubber there for padding as the bare spokes would tear my thumbs up. When I did Sebring, Daytona, Le Mans—all the long-distance races—I used to have rubber taped to the spokes where they met the wheel. It was crude but it's a lot better than chewing up your thumbs. Nowadays they make steering wheels the way they should be made.

Final preparations before taking some laps—we're making the seat nice and comfortable. An excellent time to adjust your mirrors—especially with a willing assistant handy.

Don't forget that your tires, wheels, and suspension are sending input up the steering column, right out the wheel spokes to the rim of the steering wheel to your hands. So, first, the steering wheel should be gripped firmly, but not too tightly.

No "white-knuckle-driving" please. Relax into a firm grip but don't strangle it. If you grip the wheel too tightly you will fatigue yourself and your tense muscles will cause you to make small, involuntary movements of the wheel if you are driving really hard.

If you find your grip tightening just take a deep breath. That will relax your shoulders and arms—and your whole upper body will let you feel the car better. It may sound simple, but it really works. Not just driving, but anytime. If you are tense and tight, needing to relax. Just take a deep breath. A full long inhale and exhale. Maybe once or twice. You will relax, feel better, and find that your concentration and smoothness are improved too. If you are relaxed you will definitely be a lot quicker.

Steering Wheel Hand Positions

Think of the wheel as the face of a round clock, picture where 3:00 is, put your right hand there. Fine, now picture where 9:00 is, and put your left hand there. This is what is referred to as the three-and-nine hand position. If you have a three-spoke wheel on your car, chances are the spokes run at 3:00, 6:00, and 9:00.

If your family sedan's steering wheel is too big and just has one huge bar across the center(and your hands keep slipping on the plastic), you might want to get an aftermarket steering wheel that's padded and covered in leather to make it less slippery and give you better car feel and control.

Most of the new cars today have good

Just a quick glance in the mirror lets you know what's going on behind you—with a driver like the late Graham Hill on your tail, you'd better "put the willy to it!" *Bob Tronolone*

sports steering wheels as standard equipment. They allow you to easily find a proper hand position. Many now have airbags built in to them, which usually give you a hand position of 2:30 and 9:30. This still gives you lots of control and allows you a driving position that is less fatiguing.

Now, with your hands at 3:00 and 9:00, try to make a turn keeping your hands in place without moving them all over the wheel. Now you have created one more source of input. Your thumbs resting lightly on the spokes also give you just that extra little bit of feel and leverage in hard cornering. Be sure to use the heel or the inner part of your palm on the rim of the wheel for not only input but also for strength and leverage. Your thumbs can't do the whole job.

By always gripping the wheel at the same position you always know where straight ahead is and you always know just how much steering you have put in. Knowing where straight ahead is doesn't seem that important when you are heading down a straight-away but when you're in a corner out of shape or you just lost it, that instinct and knowing where straight ahead is can really be important.

If you are going to make contact—and I mean just before an inevitable impact—take your hands from the wheel and you won't break your thumbs or wrists. When a front wheel hits a wall or another car the force usually spins the steering wheel; if you're still in a death grip, you're going to break more than just the car.

Back to input.... Another good reason for keeping your hands in one place is that the more you move them around the less time they are in contact with the steering wheel, losing the advantage of chassis information being fed in. Remember to *feel* what the car is doing through the steering wheel at all times.

If you need more steering wheel input to get around a sharp or tight corner, then slide the right hand up to the 11:00 position on the right-hand corner keeping the left hand at 9:00, so that the left hand can smoothly and precisely steer the car out of the corner. Do just the opposite on a left-hand corner, sliding the left hand up to the 1:00 position. This is important for precise cornering. If the wheel requires more input (as in a car with slower turning rates), then do a hand-over position using the thumbs under the opposite side spokes.

Mirror Adjustment

Now that you've gotten your driving position correct, your seat belts snug, your grip on the steering wheel set, let's look around. What can you see? Everything is great out the windshield and side windows. But can you see out of your mirrors? You have to know what is going on around you—both on the track and on the street.

Mirrors are there as a driving aid—use them! To be able to use them they must be adjusted properly. Take the time to do it. If you are in a racing car it will save a lot of time and aggravation to get them adjusted before you fasten your seat belts because chances are you won't be able to reach them afterward.

Mirrors are a lot easier to adjust on your street car so don't just forget or say that they are almost OK—even though you have to lean almost clear across the car to see out of the right one. Adjust them before you drive away and keep them adjusted. It is just safer.

Keep your mirrors clean too. Dirty mirrors are a real serious cause of night glare.

Some racers don't use their mirrors and some racers crash into cars trying to overtake them; so use them or you could be in trouble too!

A student of mine was so intent on watching his mirrors—especially as this other (fast and advanced) student came up on him—that he ran straight off the road. He was looking at his mirrors all the time and not watching in front of him at the upcoming turn.

Glance in the mirrors to get input as to what is going on around you. Don't stare.

Pay attention to what is in front of you but use your mirrors to tell you what to expect from behind.

Adjusting your mirrors may be the last thing you do before starting your car, but do it, and use them.

Now that you're seated properly and have your hands correctly placed on the wheel with your seat belts snug and your mirrors correctly adjusted, do you feel in control? Almost? Maybe after the next chapter.

Getting to Know the Controls

Now you've learned the importance of feeling the input from the car to you. This can't be over-emphasized. But there is another bit of input, the significance of which can't be stressed enough: the input from you, the driver, to the car.

You're all strapped in and comfortable. But before you touch that key you need to know what your hands and feet should be doing. While your hands are resting at 3:00 and 9:00, let's put your feet to work.

Foot Pedal Position and Adjustment

Important Step Number One: Make sure your feet reach the pedals, *comfortably*. This can be accomplished by adjusting the seat properly for a bent-leg and bent-arm position at the wheel. If your feet still don't reach the pedals, you can fix the pedals. It's easy in a race car, as they are usually adjustable.

In a street car it's a little more difficult but it can be done. A plate can be welded, pop-riveted or bolted onto the pedals to move them closer to you. With many cars there is room to remount the whole pedal assembly closer or farther away. As with the distance from the seat to the steering wheel, the distance from the seat to the pedals is crucial—*especially in a race car.*

Like your bent-arm driving position, you want to have a bent-leg driving position. You want to be able to reach the pedals with the balls of your feet, *not your toes.* Never have your legs so straight that you have to stretch to work the pedals with the tips of your toes.

You should be positioned so that when you have the brakes or clutch fully depressed, you still have your knees bent. What if your leg was fully extended when the brakes were on full and the pedal level dropped or the brakes started to fade during a real heated drive? You'd really be in trouble. The same goes for throttle. So, modify the car to fit the driver. You want to be able to reach everything and feel everything when you're properly seated in the car.

Like the seat, the pedals are extremely

The bent-leg driving position helps assure your ability to comfortably work all of the pedals with the balls of your feet, giving you better car feel and less fatigue.

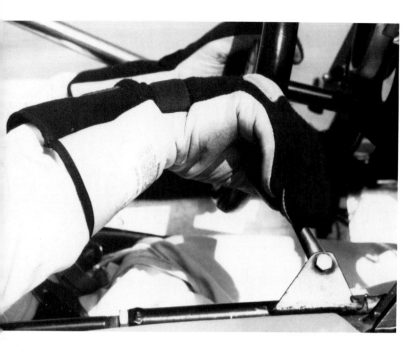

The proper hand position for shifting from first into second and third into fourth on a normal H-pattern gearbox. Treat the shift knob like an eggshell.

important in conveying what the car is doing. The ball of your foot should be used when braking or operating the clutch. It is the strongest and most sensitive part of your foot.

Clutch Pedal Position and Use

When not using the left foot (clutch foot), it should be near but not on the clutch pedal. Some cars have a "dead-pedal," or foot rest just left of the clutch, but most don't. It is important to have a place to put your left foot to help brace you during hard cornering. You want to use both the ball heel of your foot to brace yourself in the seat.

If your car has no place to brace and rest your foot, you would do well to consider putting a "dead-pedal" nearby at about the same height as the clutch pedal at rest. It's easy to do.

Brake Pedal Position and Use

Maximum braking efficiency is just

before a wheel locks up. Your foot must be taught, through practice and experience, what is the perfect pressure and what is too much.

Like all the other controls, the brake pedal should be operated smoothly—squeezed on, not jumped on.

Throttle Pedal Position and Use

The throttle must also be used smoothly. Jump on the throttle of a 427 Cobra and see where you end up!

For operating the throttle, your heel should be firmly placed on the floor. This provides a pivot point to operate the throttle with the most feel and control. It enables you to feed in the throttle in a smoother fashion. In a high-speed drift, you are delicately balanced with throttle control. Just a bit too much or too little can quickly send you off the road.

Before leaving the subject of pedals, it should be stressed that before you fire up your car be sure that your foot pedals and

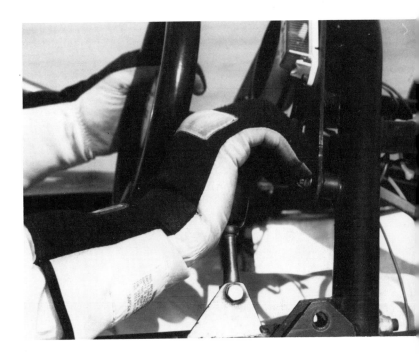

The correct position for shifting from second to third and fourth to fifth: use your wrist and gently guide the lever with the heel and palm of your hand. Smooth, clean shifts are much more important than fast shifts.

the bottom of your driving shoes (street shoes, too) are dry and clean. It is distracting and dangerous if your shoes or pedals are slippery or wet. If your shoe slips off the brake in the middle of the pack on the first lap, coming into the first corner at 100+ mph, you are in for a lesson you'd be better off without. The same thing applies in street traffic.

Gearshift Position and Use

Shifting is one of the most basic things about driving a car. Shifting up to a higher gear is easy, but many people even do that incorrectly.

You should treat the gearshift lever like it was a fresh raw egg. By that I mean, don't strangle or attack it, don't slam it from gear to gear—you'll have egg all over your hand. Cup the palm of your hand over the top of the lever and let your fingers extend down the lever shaft to provide guidance.

Secrets of Upshifting

With a typical four- or five-speed-forward gearbox you'll have a basic H-pattern shift arrangement (with the fifth gear placed usually to the upper right, above reverse). To shift from first to second, place the cupped palm of your hand on the lever, palm covering the knob, fingers down and use them to guide the lever back into second, gently.

From second to third, just use the heel of the palm and the wrist, making sure to give it the necessary movement to the right at the neutral gate. Do it gently and smoothly; don't slam it.

For the shift from third to fourth, again use the fingers and the wrist to guide it back; and for fourth to fifth again use the heel to guide it up. You want to be firm and positive, but still gentle and smooth. Remember to always use a gentle hand and wrist action, not a "death grip" and strong arm.

I learned this method of shifting quite

by accident. I was driving a BRM Formula 1 car that was set up for a smaller driver. My arms were considerably longer and the only way I could get it in gear was to use a wrist action and the palm of my hand and my fingers because there was so little room in the cockpit. It worked so well I kept on doing it.

Before that I, like most others, was trying to force it into gear and making a fist around the lever. As it turned out, I was doing it right by mistake, and it was not only easier but it really saved the gearboxes as well.

You should treat the gearshift lever like it was a fresh raw egg. By that I mean, don't strangle or attack it, don't slam it from gear to gear—you'll have egg all over your hand.

It's not easy. You're steering with one hand, working the pedals with both feet, and also paying attention to what's going on around you because...

...some joker may be putting a move on you.

Speed in shifting is not really as important as a good clean shift. Not much is gained with a real fast shift, and it may cost you a transmission. Many transmissions and shifting linkage just won't be shifted fast. They require a slight hesitation at the neutral gate or they grind. In a proper race car the gearbox is designed much differently and the gears are straight cut and without synchromesh so you really have to be smooth and precise. In a race car you must shift quickly and at the right rpm but you also must be smooth and gentle so the gearbox lasts. In all of your driving be smooth and gentle on your car and it will be that much more reliable and fun to drive.

Secrets of Downshifting

Proper heel and toe downshifting is just as important on the street as in racing—especially in wet weather so as not to lock up your drive wheels and go for a spin. In front-wheel-drive cars, if you lock up your front wheels you also lose your steering momentarily, which can be pretty hairy too.

Proper downshifting is important not just in going fast but also in driving your car to its full potential. Unless you learn to downshift correctly you will never go really quick.

Proper downshifting is not easy. It requires lots of coordination, concentration, and practice. This is the time to get everything working together: both hands, both feet, and most important (and most difficult for some), your mind. Your left hand is steering, your right hand is shifting, your left foot is working the clutch, and your right foot is not only braking but also rolling on and off the throttle , and your mind is telling you to keep up the proper revs. That's not all: your ears are listening

to the engine and gearbox sounds; your eyes are looking for your turn-in point for the corner, at your tach, and maybe at the car in your mirror.

All of this is happening at the same time and to make things even a bit worse, there's even more going on. Entering a corner you may be trying to pass someone or the driver behind you might be putting a move on you, you may be trying to avoid some oil, another car spinning, or trying to keep from spinning yourself. Maybe all of this at once. An awful lot is going on and you've just been introduced to heel-and-toe downshifting.

Fortunately, on the street it is a little easier than on the racetrack but the procedure to carry out a proper downshift is the same. The best way to learn your shifting and heel-and-toe downshifting is to practice it (a lot) before you ever turn your car on or roll it out of the garage. If you can't do it right sitting still then you'll never get it right with the car moving. After you've mastered it in the garage, practice it on the street; getting it perfected on the racetrack will then be easy.

I find that the first problem that my students have with heel-and-toe downshifting is a misconception. Many think that an important reason for downshifting is to take advantage of the engine's braking effect. That thought has somehow survived from the days of skinny tires, fat drivers, and rapidly fading drum brakes. Modern ventilated disc brakes have really changed that. With the great stopping power of modern brakes it is unnecessary and with high-stressed modern engines it is a good way to break them.

In racing, rev-limiters only work during acceleration, not during deceleration. That is, they cut the motor out at a fixed rev-limit while under acceleration, but

Outlined in this series of photographs is the correct technique for the heel-and-toe double-clutch sequence.

Coming into the corner, you are under acceleration with the ball of your right foot on the throttle and your left foot at rest.

Your right foot squeezes on the brakes, slowing the car and transferring the weight forward onto the front tires. Your left foot readies for the double-clutch and the shift. The clutch is not yet depressed.

Your left foot depresses the clutch with the ball of your foot. Your right foot, which is still braking, pivots and rolls over onto the throttle to rev the engine as the clutch is going in. Your shift is passing through the neutral position.

Your left foot releases the clutch halfway. Your right foot continues braking with the throttle still on. The shift passes through neutral.

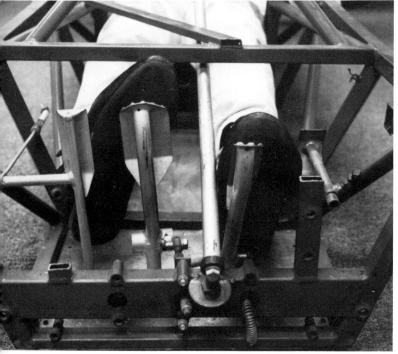

Your left foot fully depresses the clutch with the ball of your foot. Your right foot continues braking with the throttle now at your desired rpm. The shift is completed into the lower gear.

Your left foot releases the clutch smoothly as the shift is completed and the throttle is released as the clutch plate takes hold. Your right foot pivots off the throttle and starts trail-braking.

As the trail-braking is completed, your right foot is back on the throttle.

when a downshift is made at too high of an rpm the engine has no choice but to over-rev if the clutch has been let out too soon and proper braking hasn't been completed to balance the gear and engine speeds. If you over-rev, you may not break the engine right at that moment, but maybe a valve will be bent or stretched, and before long it will show up and you'll need a rebuild, probably not even realizing why.

The goal when downshifting is to change to a lower gear while maintaining maximum braking, without upsetting the car's weight transfer and balance. To do this there must be a perfect match between engine, gearbox, and rear wheel rpm (or the front wheel rpm on a front-wheel-drive car), which requires your foot to do "double-duty."

The technique required is called "heel-and-toe." Heel-and-toe is something of a misnomer. The term actually was started in the 1950s with Ferrari. Once, at Riverside, I was testing a 4.9 liter Ferrari and the pedals were actually set up for doing a true heel-and-toe. It was really a different pedal arrangement; the clutch was on the left like it should be, but the throttle was in the middle and the brake was on the right. The reason was the brakes in those days didn't stop well, unlike today. So it took a lot more muscle and foot pressure to slow it down. With that car you could literally operate the gas with the heel while you pressed the brake with your toe or the ball of your foot. It seemed logical but the pedal arrangement didn't last too long as it was just opposite to the normal procedure on all of the other production cars. I thought it was OK until one time I was entering the high-speed Turn Nine at Riverside and forgot which was where for a second and I near-

ly crashed. I prefer the normal setup. This pedal arrangement has long since disappeared but the name has survived.

As previously discussed, you should brake with the ball of your right foot, *not your toes*, and this goes equally for proper heel-and-toe.

Secrets of Double-Clutching

Heel-and-toe is a function of downshifting, so along with this, the procedure of "double-clutching" is used at the same time—the British refer to it as "double-declutching." Double-clutching can be done on the upshift as well as on the downshift but it is generally thought of as a downshift function.

To double-clutch by itself is a rather simple procedure. First you push in the clutch, move the gear shift lever out of gear and into the neutral gate, release the clutch about halfway, then depress it again *instantly*, then continue your shift to the next desired gear, and let the clutch out.

Secrets of Heel-and-Toe Shifting

Now, to heel-and-toe. First, the simple description of it alone, then we'll combine it with double-clutching, and you'll have the complete downshift.

The simple function of the right foot in heel-and-toe is to, with the ball of your foot, brake for any given corner. Now comes the tricky part. At the same time your braking is being accomplished it is necessary to also rev the engine a predetermined amount with the right side of your right foot so that the clutching and shifting procedure can be accomplished at the same time.

In simple terms, while braking with the ball of your right foot, the heel pivots to the right, still maintaining full braking pressure, and squeezes the throttle the proper amount of revs, then pivots back under the brake pedal to finish the braking or trail-braking procedure.

Now for the combined function, we'll move from fourth gear to third gear, a simple, straightforward downshift, but the procedure is the same with any gear combination.

1) Start your braking procedure. Use the ball of your right foot, squeezing on the brake, increasing the pressure as necessary. Have your left foot in position to depress the clutch. (Don't push it in yet, just be ready.)

2) Move your hand to the shift lever—just the palm of your hand cupped over the shift knob with your fingers extending down the shaft. Continue your braking. Now push in your clutch and move the shift lever from fourth to the neutral gate. As your clutch goes in, pivot your right heel and roll the side of your right foot onto the throttle.

3) Continue braking, while letting the clutch out halfway (double-clutching), squeeze on the throttle with the side of your right fool, and rev up to a level just above where it was in fourth gear ready to shift down to third, about 4000rpm in most cars.

4) Continue braking, push in the clutch again, and complete the shift. Pivot and roll your right heel back under the brake pedal completely after finishing the shift from neutral to third. As you ease the clutch back out, keep trailing the brake through the first third of the corner to maintain the chassis set.

5) The clutch plates have taken hold and the revs weren't too high nor too low—just nice and smooth. Continue braking and start to turn into the corner, gradually easing pressure off the brakes by

a third of the way into the corner (trail-braking). Then you can smoothly bring in the throttle, accelerate through the apex area and out of the turn. Smooth.

The moral is: Use the brakes to help you steer into a corner and use the throttle to help you steer out of a corner.

As mentioned before, it's best to practice with the car parked first. It seems like a lot of things to do in a short time but you'll get so you can do the whole operation in little more than one second, maybe even less.

The revving of the throttle is important during the procedure. The amount of revs somewhat depends on the individual car but the important thing is to match the speed of the engine to that of the drive wheels (front-drive or rear-drive, it doesn't matter). If the clutch is engaged with the rpm too low the drive wheels will lock up causing a skid. The best that can happen is you will mess up the corner. The worst is you might damage your drivetrain, spin out, crash, or all of the above.

If you have too many rpm when you let the clutch out the car will be forced into acceleration, transferring the weight to the rear with driving force (the engine is usually more powerful than the brakes) so you can push right off the turn. The best place to begin practicing is in an empty parking lot: not fast, just practice until you feel confident. Don't worry, it'll come!

The real key to doing this right is first that the engine rpm is matched with the drive wheel rpm when the gear change is made and second that the clutch is released positively and smoothly. Don't pop it out and don't slip it. Just be smooth.

With some responsive street cars you want to squeeze the throttle and hold it until the shift is complete. Then as you ease the clutch out, ease off the throttle

Many drivers think that an important reason for downshifting is to take advantage of the engine's braking effect. That thought has somehow survived from the days of skinny tires, fat drivers, and rapidly fading drum brakes. Modern ventilated disc brakes have really changed that.

smoothly as the clutch is taking hold, for a smooth shift.

Maximizing Brake and Throttle Pedal Setup

Of course, to heel-and-toe properly, the car must be set up correctly. That is to say, the throttle and the brake pedal must be arranged in a proximity to each other so when the brakes are fully compressed, the brake pedal is still slightly higher and directly adjacent to the throttle.

One problem you can experience is brake fade and a drop in pedal level. If your pedal level drops significantly during a heel-and-toe operation it is likely that you will inadvertently accelerate at the same time you are braking by catching your ankle on the side of the throttle pedal. This can be detrimental to your braking effort! One solution is to learn to double-pump your brake pedal to bring it back up

Smoothness is imperative—especially when controlling cars with high horsepower-to-weight ratios such as this Cobra Daytona Coupe. You really had to be aggressively smooth. We ran 196mph down the Mulsanne straight at Le Mans in 1965. *Bernard Cahier*

to pressure. But the best method is, like all parts of your car, to make sure your brakes are in good order and that you won't experience a brake fade or unexpected problems.

To repeat, practice heel-and-toe with the car stopped and the motor off before you try it on the road. Get it down while you aren't moving in traffic.

One more word of caution: If you have a carbureted engine (not fuel injection), chances are that while you sit in your car practicing the heel-and-toe and double-clutching you'll probably flood your engine and have trouble starting it after a half-hour of practice. Let the car sit for a few minutes so you can let the raw fuel evaporate. Then start the engine. If you have trouble starting the engine at that time, press the throttle to the floor and hold it there till the engine starts. If you have fuel injection you won't have *that* problem because it only operates when the ignition (key) is on.

Automatic Transmission Shifting

How about an automatic? Jim Hall's Chaparral had one, so do the Williams, Ferrari, and McLaren Formula 1 cars— maybe your BMW or Ferrari has one too.

Most people put their automatic transmission in drive and leave it there forever, except to back up. Use the gears, that's what they are there for. For accelerating, use each of the gears, wind it out. Make the car work as it was intended to.

As for downshifting, you can't heel-and-toe, but your braking procedure is still the same. Use the ball of your foot and trail the brake into the first third of the corner, just like if you were driving a stick-shift. When you've braked sufficiently for a downshift, move the lever to the gear you want and wait for the transmission to

shift itself down, transferring the weight back to the rear of the car. This could help your braking, but remember to slow the car with the brakes, not with the engine. And when you accelerate, just ease on the gas.

With an automatic in top gear (drive) the engine back pressure (slowing force) is minimal, you only use this back pressure in the lower gears. For example, coming down a steep grade you should use your engine and it will help to reduce brake fade. In cornering, the lower gears of an automatic help the car's stability and responsiveness. Rather than using drive, use an appropriate lower gear along with the throttle and the car will steer around a corner much easier and safer.

Left-Foot Braking

I don't recommend left-foot braking unless you learned it when you first learned to drive and have continued from that time on. You're using the throttle all of the time with the right foot and you develop a real delicate touch and feel with that foot that carries over to your braking, too. If all of a sudden, without a lot of previous practice, you start using your left foot on the brake you'll find that you haven't developed the needed sensitivity and you'll be locking up the brakes or not depressing them sufficiently to stop in time, especially in emergency situations. In the Chaparrals and the Williams it worked OK but you weren't dealing with power brakes—and the drivers like Phil Hill and Nigel Mansell were world champions too....

When I ran Indy, you had left-foot braking so I had to practice especially for that technique. I practiced with an automatic and left-foot braking for two solid months before I ever got into the Indy car.

Left-foot braking is really different depending on which way the corner goes. In a left-hand corner, it can work pretty well because your right heel is on the floor bracing your body. In this direction, you are not upsetting your body position in the feel of the car and you can meter the brake on quite nicely with the left foot.

A right-hand corner is a different story. Your body tends to fall to the left in a right-hand corner and if you are trying to left-foot brake you are also putting your weight on your left heel on the floor while trying to brake. It doesn't work so well and it's just not as smooth. You need to brace yourself in the car with your left foot, which makes a big difference.

You can practice and make it work but unless you have a real definite reason to brake with your left foot, I wouldn't bother. I'll bet if you get into any kind of emergency situation you'll end up stomping on the brakes, lock the front wheels up—and all of a sudden you've lost your steering and you'll be plowing the field. Use your practice time wisely...but you have to make the final decisions.

As you've figured out by now, downshifting is not easy to master and once you do learn to get it right, you need a lot of practice and attention. The best thing about shifting is that it can be practiced every day in your normal driving.

To go really quickly you have to get all of the parts to work together. Practice them. Give them your time and your attention. Feeling more comfortable behind the wheel now? Great. Now let's get to know your car even better.

Getting to Know Your Car

Your car's particular balance is monitored by the tires, steering, and chassis. Your seating and steering-wheel position are vitally important because these are your sensor probes, telling you just what your car is doing at all times. These sensor probes enable you to make full use of the entire 100 percent of theoretical traction limit available.

Car Preparation

To make full use of all your sensors, you must have faith that your car is giving you correct input. This means that your car must be properly prepared and maintained. The value of proper preparation and maintenance really pays off. You will have fewer problems, more enjoyable driving, and a substantial savings of money. Proper maintenance will catch most costly repairs early enough to keep them minimal. Fix it before it is broken, don't wait until it's too late.

When racing the BRM Formula 1 car, I was confronted with the problem of maintenance. At the Nürburgring, I was having a great battle going with the factory Ferraris of Lorenzo Bandini, Ludovico Scarfiotti, and Mike Parkes, when a camshaft broke. I missed the next race, the Dutch Grand Prix, because the engine was being rebuilt and it didn't get finished in time (two engines would have been a luxury for the under-financed team).

The car arrived at Monza "ready to race." I found that the only thing that had been touched on the car was the re-installation of the engine. At Nürburgring it had rained during the whole race. When I looked over the car, it was covered with spots of rust.

I couldn't believe it! All they did was take the engine out, push it into a corner, and when the engine came back, they just put it back in. They hadn't touched the car other than that. So, I walked around the car, found a few nuts that were a half-turn loose, a few more a full-turn loose and some that were missing entirely. I was disgusted. I grabbed a handful of wrenches and went over the entire car. I reset the chassis and tightened every nut and bolt.

Airborne at Germany's Nürburgring in 1966 shortly before the broken camshaft put me out of the race while running in fourth, battling the factory Ferraris. *Foto-Kraling*

It didn't go well that day. I really didn't trust that car, as no one had maintained it. During the race I could never get the car going up to full potential. I think I ran about ninth. That was my last ride with that team. Seeing that things weren't going to get any better, and not being able to trust the team or the car, after the race I quit.

Proper preparation of your car is vital, be it a racing car or the family sedan. In racing, a driver is certainly not going to win unless he or she finishes. A well-maintained car is a must. The costs of having a car properly maintained and prepared are high, but not as high as letting it go. Assuming that you have a certain amount of mechanical competency, do as much of the maintenance and preparation as you can. This goes for both the street or the racetrack. The better that you know your car the better driver you will become. If you know nothing of mechanics

then try to find the time to take a class at your local college or high school—you are investing in yourself.

Tools and Workspace

Before you attempt to work on your car, make sure you have a complete set of the necessary tools. In addition to the standard tools make sure that you have the specialized ones required for your particular car. Nothing is more discouraging than wasting an hour to do something that, with the proper tool, could have been done in an minute. Of great importance: be sure to buy quality tools. A cheap wrench or socket will spread or round. It can do expensive damage to the part you are trying to fix.

While you are becoming a first-rate mechanic, with meticulous work habits and good tools, it is also important to have a good place in which to work. Nothing, and I mean nothing, can make working on your car more unpleasant than a cramped, cold, dirty, and poorly lit work area. Try to have a place that has enough room, is clean (like your car needs to be), plenty of light, and is well heated to make what you are doing both easier and more pleasurable. Preparing a race car will take lots of hours; make sure your investment is secure in a properly laid out, well lit, clean, and warm work area. Those preparation hours will be both much more pleasant and definitely more productive.

When preparing a race car (not a bad idea for maintaining a street car either), use check lists such as these:

1) A specific list of work to do on the car:
   A) Routine checks and maintenance
   B) Repairs to be done
   C) Potential trouble spots to be checked
2) A standard list of each step in the preparation process
3) A list of each item that you will be taking with you to the races

Without check lists, trying to prepare a race car and getting it to the track with everything you need can be a chaotic undertaking. Race car or street car, small problems left unattended have a way of producing major consequences. A leaking fuel line, little hang-ups in the throttle linkage, a decreasing brake fluid reservoir—all these things and many more can lead to expensive confrontations of one kind or another.

Safety, Reliability, and Performance

If you work a full-time job and do all of your own car preparation and maintenance then your time will be at a premium. Work on a priority basis. First, take care of everything that could adversely affect your car's *safety*. Then concentrate on those things that will affect your car's *reliability*. Your last concern should be with modifications for *performance*.

If you are preparing for racing, what wins is meticulous and methodical preparation to ensure that your car functions properly. There is no black magic involved.

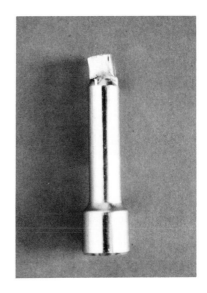

Good-quality tools—always! Imagine trying to get an accurate torque reading using this socket wrench extension.

Meticulous preparation pays off not only in a good-looking race car but one that will be reliable—especially important on a high-stress course like Italy's Monza. This Ferrari Dino was fantastically prepared—a car you could really feel confident at the limit.

A large distinction should be made between race car preparation and race car development. The major expenditure in race car preparation is time. The major expenditure in race car development is money. Of course, time is money but in development it takes a lot of time in addition to a lot of money.

If you are interested in race car preparation, then I recommend a book that was written by Carroll Smith, Shelby's crew chief for the factory Cobras and GT 40s. It is titled *Prepare to Win,* and it is excellent. Smith's book outlines step by step what should be done, how it should be done, and what tools are necessary to properly prepare a racing car. Required reading!

Performance modifications and having the "trickest" car at the circuit are neat, but they are also expensive. Also, if you are continually trying new trick parts there is a good chance that you won't know how your car should be actually running or handling and you won't know where to pinpoint your troubles because of confused or mixed input coming back to you.

What you should be primarily concerned with is learning how to drive your car the best that you can. If you are on a tight budget, use the money to become a first-class driver. Keep your car clean and well maintained; but if it comes to a choice of $200 for a trick part or $200 for a day of practice, spend the money on practicing. In a year or two that car will probably be sold and you'll have a faster, tricker, and better one, but your skill as a driver will always be with you. Invest in yourself...it always stays with you.

It is important to have a car that is properly maintained so that it can be depended on to react in the same fashion each time it is called on to do so. By doing your own maintenance and preparation, and doing it thoroughly, you know your car better and can trust it more completely.

Along with good maintenance goes cleanliness. Keep the car clean—not simply the outside, but keep it clean in the engine compartment and underneath too. Don't let dirt built up. If it does, you won't be able to spot a crack in the chassis, a loose nut or bolt, or an oil leak. You have to be able to tell where that oil leak is coming from. It may be from the pan, a main seal, oil filter gasket, or maybe your sump plug is about to fall out and dump all your oil on the track.

To get to know your car well takes a lot of time learning and checking everything but it pays off. Your mind will be at ease and you can concentrate on driving, not worrying about what's going to fall off next or if the brakes are going to work at the next turn. If you know your car well and can trust it and its preparation, you'll be miles ahead of the competition. And that goes for both the street and the race-track.

If you are preparing for racing, what wins is meticulous and methodical preparation to ensure that your car functions properly. There is no black magic involved.

A well-lit, well-equipped workplace is essential: here's a couple of my road cars being tuned and prepared for classes.

Cleanliness is key to a good-running operation: here's one of my meticulous workers sweeping out the Formula Ford garage.

Getting to Know Yourself

Making your car perform up to its full potential takes a total effort. The delicate balance between braking, cornering, and acceleration is a balance of self.

This balance, as you learn and practice it, permits you to recognize and maintain 100 percent car control at all times. Every bit of practice, on the street or the racetrack, helps to facilitate a full and complete blending of functions, ultimately arriving at precise control of the car. The old adage, "Practice makes perfect" is correct when it comes to driving. Practice builds smoothness and consistency but they are governed by a important element that enables it all to happen: *concentration*.

Perfecting Your Concentration

While driving on the street, there are many distractions that constantly bombard your concentration. At normal speeds these lapses are into the never-never land of radios, CDs, cellular telephones, billboards, neat-looking cars, attractive pedestrians, and hundreds of other distractions to your concentration. On the street, usually all that happens is you slow down to take it all in. The possibility of a fender-bender is an everpresent danger if you really become occupied with something that distracts you from your driving. That's on the street.... It's a lot different on the racetrack.

In racing concentration is an absolute must. There is no other way if you are to be successful and at the same time safe. A slight lapse in concentration for just a moment, even a *fraction of a second*, can cause you to miss a shift or an apex, spin, blow an engine, or crash. If you lose concentration all of this can happen—and more. Most top racing teams have radio communication with the drivers, but most only allow the driver to talk to the team, not the team to the driver so that his or her concentration is not broken by such a distraction.

As important as your concentration is, it is no guarantee that you will go fast. Your concentration may be flawless but you may be doing the same thing wrong

in precisely the same way, time after time. Practice building concentration. Then concentrate on the proper way to drive and on being consistently smooth. Your ultimate goal is this equation:

Concentration + Technique + Preciseness + Consistency = Smoothness

The Ultimate Goal: Smoothness

Smoothness takes a lot of self-discipline. But smooth is fast, and smooth is safe. Smoothness is more than just an aspect of technique, it is virtually a state of mind. Cars respond positively to firm, consistent, and gentle treatment.

Smoothness is not doing just one thing smooth, but everything. It is the way you handle the steering wheel, the relaxed but alert way you sit, the way you squeeze on or ease off the brakes or the throttle. It is the precise way you change gears and the

sensitivity you have to everything your car is doing under you. Anyone can do it but some just do it better. Some have more sensitivity and feel and are just naturally smoother. But lots of practice and good instruction can only make you better. When driving slowly it is not as noticeable but when driving a high-performance car fast, smoothness really makes a difference in how fast you go.

The most difficult factor in the equation is consistency. All that you do while driving a car is interrelated. If you are inconsistent or erratic in just one aspect of your driving it will negatively affect all the rest. Consequently smoothness is lost. Smoothness is the sum total of everything you do while driving. A *positive attitude* is a must.

Smoothness is derived from sensitivity, prolonged by consistency, and made possible by unrelenting concentration and car feel! If you want to race, smoothness is helpful...if you want to win, it's *essential*.

I remember when the late Dave MacDonald and I were racing against each other in Corvettes. Dave was fast, one of the fastest drivers around. But he would be slipping and sliding all over the track, spending about as much time going sideways as he did going in a straight line. Part of it was his car but most of it was his style. Dave and I both went about the same speed most of the time. If Dave would have refined and smoothed out his style I know that he would have been able to go even that much faster. He was a great natural talent.

Natural talent is having a certain sense and feel about the control of a car. An up-and-coming young driver who exhibits a lot of natural talent is Mika Hakkinen. It's having the control over your own emotions and the discipline to drive with complete car feel.

Motor racing is an extremely disciplined sport, and it's really hard not to let yourself slip into the area of driving with a lot of oversteer. Oversteer is great fun but usually not as fast as if you drove smooth and clean. It's really fun to pitch a car sideways and it really looks neat but it's just not as fast.

With today's tires and their ultra-sticky compounds, their adhesion capabilities will cause oversteer a lot sooner with hard driving. The older and harder compounds (still used for many vintage race cars) allowed you to get away with a lot more oversteer without damaging your tires. Today, you have to pace yourself more to take better care of your tires if you want to do well. Which means you have to be even smoother at the controls than with earlier race cars.

Early on, drivers like Ayrton Senna and Nigel Mansell learned how to control their cars in adverse conditions, when

If you want to win, smoothness is essential. And winning can be great! *Ken Parker*

their cars or tires didn't work well or their cars just couldn't be set up properly. But later in their careers they became much smoother and even more precise driving at the absolute limit—perhaps even a fraction past their car's limit because of their great control.

As you go quicker and quicker and as cars become better and better, the margin of control becomes much finer. That's where the self-discipline comes in. You must have the delicate feel for keeping the car at the balance point. The bottom line is that even natural talent still has to be trained. It has to mature. You still have to learn, to perfect, and to refine.

You Have to Finish to Win

Just because you see a stab-and-steer driver going the same speed or faster than a smoother driver it doesn't mean that the

Smoothness is more than just an aspect of technique, it is virtually a state of mind.

two styles are equally effective. All it means is that the stab-and-steer driver is driving well below his or her potential and could be going even quicker. If speed and safety aren't reason enough, driving smooth is also much more reliable, it usually gets you there to the finish.

When you look at the records of some of the world's best drivers you will notice that they had an exceptionally high finish-

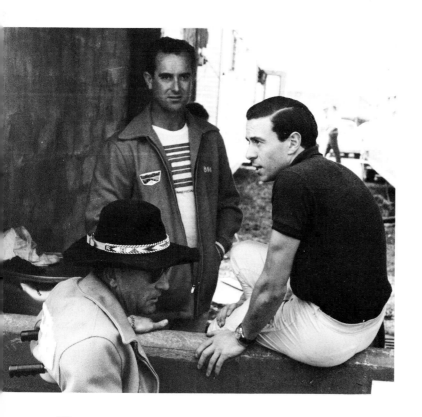

Taken at Sebring in 1964, here I am with Carroll Shelby and the great Jimmy Clark. Jimmy won two World Championships, the Indy 500, and more than a third of his Formula 1 races—not just finished, but won! He was smoothness and consistency personified as well as the real master of trail-braking. *Dave Friedman*

ing rate. Drivers like Juan Manuel Fangio, Jackie Stewart, the late Jim Clark, Alain Prost, and Ayrton Senna have not just been fast, their finish records have been fantastic. Fangio competed in fifty-one Grands Prix and won twenty-four of them, five World Championships, and averaged 5.44 world championship points per race in which he competed. That's not too bad when you consider that all you got for a win was nine points. Stewart won twenty-seven out of ninety races, three World Championships, and averaged 3.64 points per race. Clark won twenty-five out of seventy-two races, two World Championships, and averaged 3.81 points per race. Consistency is a characteristic of great competitors.

Of the more current drivers Prost and Senna stand out. Prost contested 184 Grands Prix, won three World Championships, finished in the points 62.5 percent of the time, and in the top three positions 51.09 percent of those events with an average of 3.80 points per race. Senna has shown a similar consistency with three World Championships out of 126 events contested, in the points 61.11 percent of the time, and finished in the top three 52.38 percent with an average of 3.90 points per race.

Finishing records speak for themselves. Finishing in the points (the top six positions) is an even harder achievement. Carlos Reutemann holds the all time record for consecutive races finished in the points: fifteen in a row. This spanned two seasons of racing, 1980 and 1981. Fangio comes second with fourteen straight in three seasons, 1953, 1954, and 1955. Clark reached twelve in a row and Niki Lauda eleven without a miss. Like they say you can't win if you don't finish.

You must be smooth and consistent to finish.

Setting a Regime for Practicing

A smooth, fluid driver who effortlessly blends one function into the next is easy on his or her car, saving it unnecessary stress and wear. The brakes, engine, transmission, suspension—the entire car—have a better chance of lasting if you are smooth. That is just as important for driving on the street. Make your car last.

To develop good concentration, proper technique and the all important smoothness requires practice, practice, practice. Just like when you took piano lessons as a kid. Practice whenever you drive. If you are a racer, use the time you drive on the street as practice. I don't mean blasting around town at high speed, but do take the time when you drive to practice your smoothness and concentrate on what you need to improve. It is easy to improve your braking and downshifting, double-clutching and heel-and-toe shifting while on the street. It is also a good place to practice cornering—not by going excessively fast but just by doing it properly, trail-braking, *looking ahead* for the proper apex and exit.

I was to drive the Germany's Freiburg hill climb that was one of the FIA World Manufacturers' Championship events. I'd never run a hill climb before and this road was a normal highway that would be blocked off for the hill climb on race day only. I was to drive the Cobra, but there was no way I could before the event.

I wanted to get to know the road so I took the little VW Bug that I had and every morning for about a week before, about 5a.m. I drove up and down the hill. It was a real rough climb, lots of sharp bends and it ran for about eight miles. I

Always focus your eyes ahead, where you want to go. Input from your eyes is your number one source of information.

made diagrams of it each time both up and down the hill so I could study it after I was finished driving each day. Even though I was driving the little VW, what I did was to think and to react and to put in my mind what the Cobra would be like at all the different parts of the course—where it would understeer, where it would oversteer, where it would four-wheel drift, where it would be light. I was amazed at how much I learned flogging that little VW up that hill. It was a challenge of mind, not of speed. I timed myself each run so I could see my improvement.

Smoothness is the work of methodically blending functions. In the beginning it is infinitely more important to be smooth than to be quick. Quick comes later. Concentrate on learning to drive smoothly and properly before concerning yourself with quick.

When you first try to make all the functions blend together you'll probably feel like a cow on ice. Don't be discour-

aged and don't worry about speed or how long it takes you to develop the skill. You must learn how to go smooth slowly before you will ever go smooth quickly. It takes a lot of time and it is difficult to achieve. That's probably the reason that so few drivers ever really accomplish it.

Enhancing Hand-Eye Coordination

A major part in achieving this smoothness is your *hand-eye coordination*. Your eyes are extremely important. Certainly you can steer the car with your hands and arms but *your eyes tell you where you are going—your eyes actually lead your physical movement.*

Your hands act upon the information that your eyes feed them. Focus your eyes where you want to go not where you are, or where you *don't* want to go. Look ahead; don't drive off the nose of your car. Focus all of the time on what's happening ahead so you have plenty of time to make the necessary corrections to the car if there is an emergency. If there is a turn coming up, you have to have the proper time to read how to enter it.

Train yourself to look well ahead down the road (on the street or the racetrack) and as far ahead around an approaching corner as possible. Don't just keep your focus there. You must vary it. Give yourself a visual range of three to five car lengths then out fifty or 100 yards or more. If there is a car in front of you look through its rear window and windshield to see what is happening ahead. Also, try using the vision out of your quarter windows to see further around a corner, not just through your windshield. Check your mirrors all the time so you know what's happening beside and behind you as well. *You must take it all in. You must see it all.* The more you practice the more you will see.

Good hand-eye coordination is a skill that is developed through practice. The more you can practice it, the better it will become. There are exercises that you can do with your eyes to improve them and what they tell you. There are also many activities, sports, and games that will, while affording you a good time, improve your coordination and at the same time, your physical condition.

For the eye exercises, contact your eye doctor for recommendations to improve your vision and the strength of your eyes. There are exercises that will increase your peripheral vision and others to improve your eye muscles. Keep them strong—they are your number one source of information.

As for coordination, sports such as handball, racket ball, tennis, ping pong, and the like do a lot to help improve coordination and reaction time. All of them enhance your driving skills. They all involve the basic physical requirements for driving and racing; endurance, balance, fast reflexes, and good hand-eye and foot-eye coordination. It is just as necessary to have these assets available to you driving on the street, especially in heavy traffic or if you fancy driving the back roads hard and fast.

The stress of concentration and the strain of physical exertion can take a tremendous toll on a racing driver's body. Long, grueling races and the car's heat (especially in a closed vehicle such as the Ford GT 40 or a current NASCAR stocker) all accentuate the need to be in good physical condition. This car with its 540hp really could wear you down fast if you weren't in top shape. *Dave Friedman*

Developing Your Physical Fitness

On the racing circuit, if you are to be any good at all you must be in good shape. Good physical fitness is not just desired, it's required.

You must be in good physical, ocular, mental, and emotional shape to successfully race competitively. Driving a race car at speed is far more mentally and physically demanding than any one not involved in racing could ever imagine. Your life can depend upon your degree of fitness. Coping with g forces in cornering, working the steering or brakes while functioning at the limit in extreme heat all take strength and endurance. The heat generated by a racing car through levels of a heavy driving suit amplifies the exertion required. And all the physical exertion is nothing when compared to the mental exertion.

The real sapper of strength and the primary reason for being in prime shape is the intense and unyielding concentration that you must maintain. A driver who is not fit will be worn down by the mental exertion. This produces exaggerated fatigue and that makes your concentration and coordination suffer even more. The best you can hope for is poor performance not to mention the greater possibility of an accident. And if that's not bad enough, the worse condition you are in the greater the chances are that you will be more severely injured in an accident.

The better your physical condition is, the better you will do at driving. Likewise the better you get at other sports, the better you will do in a car. You want to develop a good mental and physical condition, increase your coordination and concentration, prolong your endurance, and improve your reaction speed.

I find rowing a scull is excellent for physical conditioning. Working out with weights is also great three times a week, as well as walking one mile a day.

Pacing Yourself and Learning Your Limitations

In racing you must know where your physical and mental limitations are. Part of this can be discovered through other sports and competitive activities such as skiing, bicycling, jogging, and some weight training. In making his comeback to racing Niki Lauda spent the better part of six months improving his physical condition. He did miles of jogging and cross country skiing in addition to other exercises and regular work-outs. It made him World Champion again for the third time.

Running, especially in competition, is a lot like car racing. At the start, you push to go quickly for the first third of the race and size up the competition, see what they are going to do. You settle into a groove for the next third and keep yourself within striking distance and a good finish. The final third you push hard for a strong finish making sure you have enough left for the finish-line sprint, having paced yourself the whole way to make sure you do indeed finish. Sports and working out teach you self-discipline and how to pace yourself. It all helps you to learn your limitations and take you past them.

If you are in good physical condition you can drive long and hard and not tire. On the other hand, if you are overweight and not physically active, then you'll tire quickly. It gets hot in a race car and during a long race it is easy to lose 8–10lb just in fluids. This is demanding and exhausting. If you aren't in good condition for those kinds of demands on you body then you just won't hold up. Racing or not, get in the habit of drinking water, lots of it. Try to drink at least one or two quarts of water daily.

Endurance racing magnifies your conditioning even more. Daytona is a prime example. Recently at a twenty-four-hour event, one team had a young driver in

Video games are a good way to improve your mental speed as well as your hand-eye co-ordination.

first-class condition, while his two teammates were middle-aged and in less-than-prime shape. It wasn't a question of age, but a question of conditioning. The young, fit driver ended up doing double-duty at the wheel and finally toward morning the other two drivers quit entirely and turned their drive over to another driver who was fit enough to finish. It was an expensive waste but at least they knew better than to continue and jeopardize themselves or another driver by their fatigue.

If you want to race but are not in good physical condition, you are wasting both your time and your money. Don't impose unnecessary risks and limitations on yourself. Get in shape. It's work but it can be fun too. If you're on the road a lot try to find hotels with gyms. Working out with weights is great, as is jogging or long brisk walks. You really want to elevate your heart rate and get that blood pumping around. There are many games that can really increase your reaction speed as well as your hand-eye coordination; not just the physical sports like tennis, skiing, and handball (all of which are great for your body). A good and popular alternative that won't even break much of a sweat are video games. They are excellent for the mind, good for learning to anticipate what is coming up, and great for improving your reaction speed.

Mental conditioning is unquestionably the most important conditioning that you can do. Keep sharp, fast, and alert by keeping your mind active. When you race, you have to use strategy. Many leisure games help to promote this. Good examples are chess and backgammon as well as some of the more sophisticated computer games. These kind of games help you to make decisions—and make them quickly. One wrong decision in a race car can quickly cause you to lose, oftentimes in a big way. A delayed reaction or decision can be just as costly. Do all that you can do to improve your *total conditioning*.

Remember that your car is but a small part of driving. You are what makes the car last or what breaks it, the one who maintains it or lets it go. You are the one who learns to combine all the driving aspects into a smooth and flowing motion. You are the only one responsible for your ultimate performance. Build on yourself. Improve all that you do, physically and mentally. The more you know and the better condition you are in, the better you will become at everything. Add that to driving practice and who knows, you could become great.

Since you are your best judge and worst critic, do it for yourself. Racing is a total commitment if you are to be successful. On the street you can perhaps be a good driver even if you are a little out of shape and your reactions are a bit slow but on the track it can kill you, or someone else.

Enough lecture. Let's get out of the garage and feel what it's like to combine all your braking and shifting practice on the road. Let's try to get you into the corners—better yet, out of them—safely and quickly.

Getting Behind the Wheel

It doesn't matter what kind of car you have; if you get to know it and learn to drive it properly, it can be a great source of enjoyment. There are an increasing number of engine and drivetrain configurations on the road today—from the old tried-and-true front-engine/rear-wheel-drive setup, to front-engine/front-wheel-drive, rear-engine/rear-wheel-drive, mid-engine/rear-wheel-drive, all-wheel-drive, and even four-wheel-steering. Each performs somewhat differently and has its own handling characteristics.

What it takes is getting used to a particular car through actual driving time and practice. You must learn and remember the real basics of car control. We can give you that training of why and how cars act in a particular fashion in a given circumstance—theory backed up by practice, testing, and lots of experience.

Maximizing Traction

The key to successful high-performance driving, on the street or on the racetrack, is one easy, simple thing: *maximizing traction*. Traction is the cohesive factor between the tires and the road surface. The primary goal of a driver should be to control his or her car in a fashion to consistently take advantage of every bit of traction that is theoretically available. The basic functions of braking, shifting, cornering, and accelerating all come back to that one prime objective: *maximizing traction*.

In racing, the closer a driver gets to complete utilization of the theoretical limit of traction, the quicker he or she will go.

During the functions of braking, cornering, and acceleration, each car has its theoretical limit of traction. This limit is determined by the tires, suspension, chassis, weight, and balance of the car in addition to the abrasive level of the road surface. Notice that I first mentioned tires. The other components of this limit, each in its own way, affect the tires to either add or subtract traction.

Controlling Weight Transfer

Maximum traction is achieved by controlling weight transfer, which is, in essence, getting the shifting and moving mass of the car over the desired wheels to push those tires into maximum contact with the road.

The area of tire in contact with the road surface is referred to as the "tire contact patch." All you have between you and the road are four tire contact patches about the size of your hand. The maximum traction that you can possibly have is limited to or enhanced directly by the total tire contact patch area. It is possible to have your greatest area of traction where it is not even wanted, causing all sorts of problems in cornering and braking, not to mention those of acceleration.

Maximizing the Tire Contact Patch

When a car is sitting motionless, the largest tire contact patch areas are determined by the physical weight balance of the car. The ratio differs depending on your car's drivetrain layout:

- In a traditional front-engine and transmission/rear-wheel-drive car, the weight is normally distributed near the ratio of 50–56 percent front and 50–54 percent at the rear. This will usually give a slightly larger tire contact patch at the front than at the rear due to the slightly heavier front end.
- With a rear-engined/rear-wheel-drive car, the weight ratio usually runs 54–50 percent at the front and 56–50 percent at the rear, just about reversing the weight bias to the rear tire contact patch.
- With contemporary front-engine/front-wheel-drive cars, the weight distribution is much more forward-biased with a ratio of approximately 60–65 percent front to only 35–40 percent rear, thus making the front tire contact patches by far the largest.
- The mid-engine/rear-wheel-drive and most all-wheel-drive cars will run a near-neutral weight distribution as well as tire contact patch.

Smoothing the Weight Transfer

When you put this in motion you have added the resistance to movement of the basic weight of the car. This weight shift moves to the rear as the you accelerate, compressing the rear shocks and springs, thus adding greater weight, expanding the rear tire contact patch.

As you lift off the gas you must do it smoothly so the weight starts transferring forward to compress the front shocks and springs. Then you add smooth, even braking that further compresses the front shocks and springs, increasing the front tire contact patch. So as you start to move through the corner you now have you maximum tire contact patch providing you with your maximum adhesion. This resistance and weight movement is called weight transfer.

Weight transfer not only moves forward and backward but also laterally. In cornering, when the car is in the first third of the turn and you are maintaining a trail-brake, the weight transfer is not only coming forward but is also directed away from the center of the corner you are turning into. When turning right, the transfer of weight will be to the left front corner, increasing the tire contact patch on the left front wheel. Turning to the left, the transfer goes to the right front tire contact patch.

The balance during the transition between braking and acceleration is a delicate one because as you accelerate you are transferring the weight again to the rear. During the acceleration in a turn to the right the weight and increased tire contact patch move to the left rear; conversely, to the right rear in a left-hand turn.

This transfer of weight amplifies the need for smoothness. Any abrupt movement in weight transfer, especially at the time of transition between braking and acceleration—that is, too much too fast of either braking, lack of braking, acceleration, or lack of acceleration—will drastically alter your weight balance and, consequently, your tire contact patch, and you might find yourself going for a ride through the bushes.

Weight transfer, g forces, and momentum all work together. Weight is continually transferred as a car moves through acceleration, braking, and cornering. Your goal is to make the weight transfer harmonize with the needs of the suspension and tires to achieve optimum traction.

With a racing car you want to constantly blend your braking into cornering, your cornering into acceleration, and your acceleration into braking, keeping in mind all the time that you want to be at, but not past, the limit of maximum traction. You use the same basics on the street, but without the high speeds.

Stab-and-Steer Driving

If you are not accomplishing these transitions in one fluid motion, then you might be one of those that I refer to as the "stab-and-steer" group. Most highway drivers fall into this category if they are trying to drive fast. Likewise, the vast majority of racing drivers (and that includes many top national competitors) don't put the whole package together either—and a good per-

centage of them are also of the stab-and-steer variety.

The stab-and-steer theory is simply to go as fast as the car can go, brake as hard and as late as possible, then drive around any given corner as fast as they can, and get as much power as fast as they are able. Those guys are fun to watch and fun to photograph because their cars are always out of shape and you can expect them to run off a turn or two sometime during a race. That's fun to watch, but you must be smooth to go quick and do it consistently to win races and stay in one piece. The stab-and-steer drivers are not truly quick in terms of lap times, nor are they quick with any consistency—and they are awfully hard on their equipment.

A typical stab-and-steer driver charges into a corner, executes a late, banzai braking attempt, does a herky-jerky downshift, and jumps off the brakes (transferring the weight abruptly to the rear thereby reducing the available traction for steering). Then he or she pounds on the throttle (throwing even more weight transfer to the rear, losing even more steering control), then has to come off the throttle because the car starts to either oversteer or understeer too much (coming off the throttle transfers the weight again to the front so the steering comes back). Then they are on and off the throttle and correcting the steering all the way around the corner. This is not quick, nor is it safe.

Discovering Your Car's Limits

In the next chapter we'll detail an actual cornering sequence. The main point now is to get you to realize the importance of weight transfer because it is weight transfer that determines the amount of traction you will have available. Once you get weight transfer work-

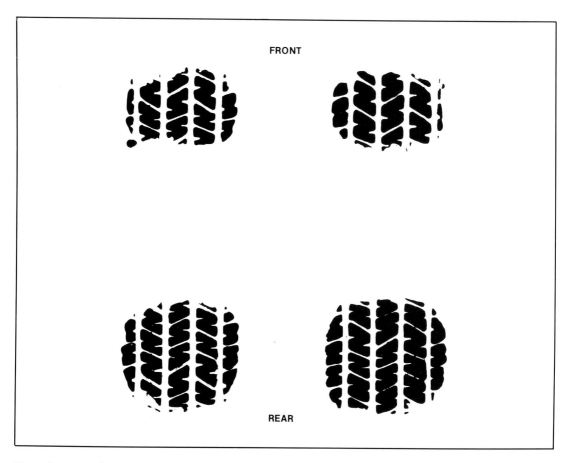

These images of tire contact patches are ideal for showing the actual effects of weight transfer on your car. This will vary slightly with the size and type of tire as well as the car, but in concept it can be used for a base of reference. These examples are from a Formula Ford, as the rear tires are larger than the front tires. This shows the car at rest.

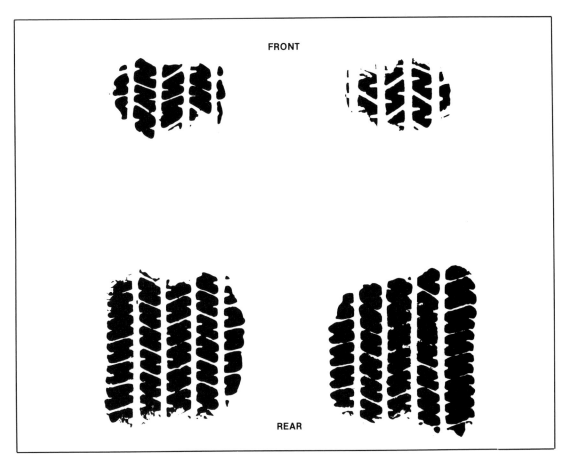

FRONT

REAR

Under acceleration the front patch has changed little—but look at the tremendous difference in the rear imprints as the weight transfers rearward.

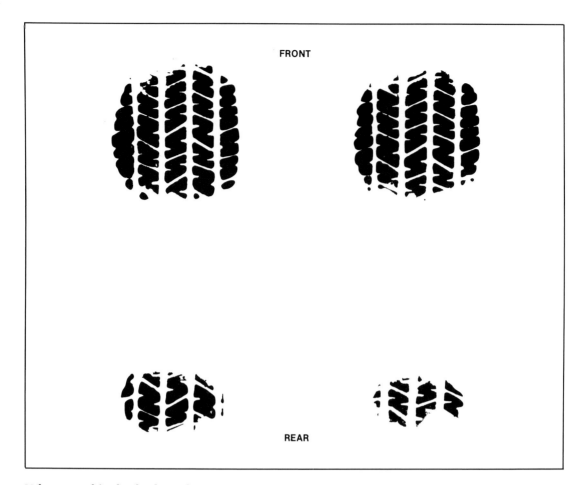

When you hit the brakes, the car's weight
shifts dramatically toward the front.

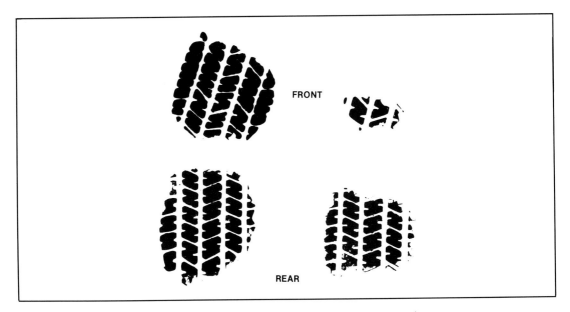

This next series of three images shows how the tire contact patches change during progress through a right-hand corner. Lateral weight transfer in a corner is pronounced.

Note that even within the left front tire patch itself, the outside (left) edge is being forced into the pavement more so than the inside edge of the tread.

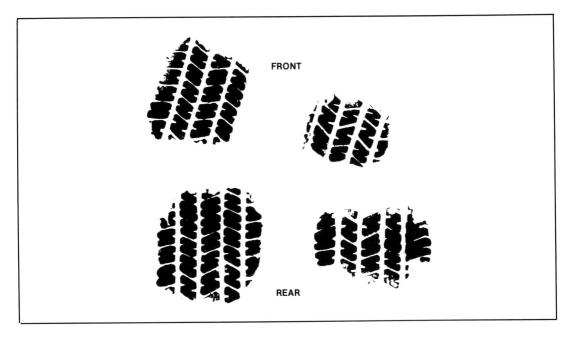

Here are the tire patches in the middle of the corner, showing a further lightening of both the front and rear inside (right) tires.

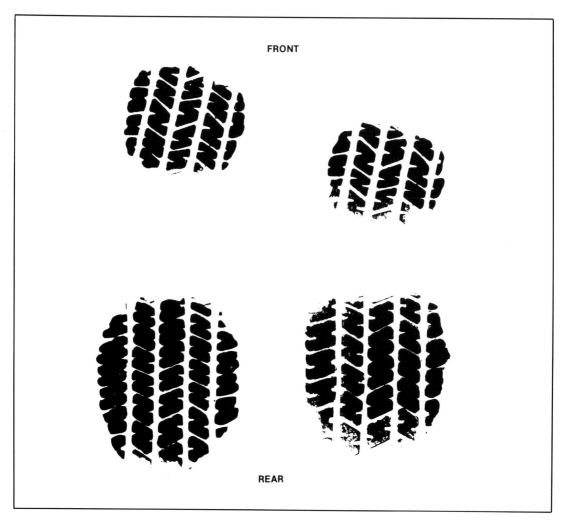

As progress is made to the exit of the corner,
all four patches begin to show weight transfer
back to a more stable position.

ing for you, you must keep it working. This is accomplished by smooth, precise, almost delicate, management of the car's controls.

As you get to know your particular car you will learn its particular balance. Learning how to drive your car the best that you can is your primary goal—the foremost reason you bought this book. To really get to know your car means lots of time behind the wheel finding out about the limits of your car and of yourself. If your car is used primarily on the street, then it's difficult as well as dangerous to find those limits. Look for competitive events such as slaloms, autocrosses, rallys, driving schools, or club outings that will allow you to find the limits of your car and yourself, safely. Discover those limits where neither you, your car, nor anyone else will get hurt.

The primary goal of a driver is smooth and consistent control and that means maximum traction!

The primary goal of a driver should be to control his or her car in a fashion to consistently take advantage of every bit of traction that is theoretically available.

Getting to Know the Road

Now that you are seated properly, holding your steering wheel correctly, have your pedals adjusted just right, have gotten yourself in good physical and mental condition, and understand the importance of maximizing traction, let's move down the road. Remember the basics: Concentrate, be smooth, precise, and consistent. If you can put all that together then you have already become a better driver than when you picked up this book.

Warming Up Your Tires

Before you get on the road, think about your tires. When you start out in the morning or any time your car has been sitting for several hours, your tires are cold. Cold tires don't make for good traction. Just ask any of the drivers who crashed after the many caution flags during the 1992 Indy 500.

Drive a few miles to warm your tires up so you'll have full traction. If the day is cold, it will take even longer. The same thing applies on the racetrack—but it's even more crucial. On a track, you can

speed the process by gently swerving back and forth in second gear during a warm-up lap. But if you are simply going out to practice, build up to speed carefully, warming up and checking out your entire car before it's time to put the pedal to the metal.

Tire Pressure

First of all, if you have a street car, with regular tires, before you even think about driving hard, make sure you have good wheel bearings and sufficient tire pressure. At my school all of the cars are run with at least 35–40psi (pounds per square inch) in each tire. Use this as a starting guide.

If you don't have enough air in the tires you can pull a tire right off the rim during hard cornering, which most likely will cause a real nasty accident. More about tires later, but make sure they have enough air; I typically run my tires at about 10psi more than the recommended street pressures or the sidewall will deflect or move and the car will feel real sloppy through the corner.

Deconstructing a Corner

Welcome, now, to the most difficult corner in the world! That reference could apply to any turn in the world as viewed by any driver. Every driver has his or her own kind of problem corners. Do you have a particular kind of corner in which you feel clumsy and slow? One you never quite feel that you got right? Do you know how to read a corner properly? How about getting it right after you read it correctly?

What is a corner anyway? Simply put, it's an entrance or an exit to a straightaway. I'm going to tell you how to do it the safest, most stable, and quickest way possible.

Any given corner can be broken up into three segments: entry, apex, and exit.

The Corner Entry

The entry to a turn is the most important part. Your entry dictates all that will follow—where, how fast, and how stable you exit. Also it is the primary factor in how fast you go down the following straightaway. The entry of the turn is where you combine braking, the double-clutch, and the heel-and-toe downshift (that you've been so diligently working on) into one fluid movement, and then make your transition into your trail-braking.

Let's concentrate on how to go through the steps of a corner properly.

I'm in a racing car and heading down the straightaway at 140mph. Ahead is a simple 90degree right-hand corner that can be completed at 90mph. As I approach the corner my eyes are feeding me input about the road, the turn, and the traffic while the input I'm receiving from the car is telling me exactly what it is doing.

As I approach the turn from the extreme left edge of the available road (about 1ft from my left wheel to the road edge) I am under full acceleration. I sight my braking point (shut-off point). I ease off the gas (don't jerk off the gas or you *pitch* the car's weight forward rather than smoothly transferring it forward), and firmly but gently squeeze on the brakes with the ball of my foot. The weight is being

Entering a late-apex area. The car is stable but in a four-wheel drift under full acceleration. All four tire patches are working at their limits. My line and my exit point are committed. *George Robitschek*

smoothly transferred to the front wheels as the springs and shocks are compressed thus increasing the tire contact patches traction. I apply maximum brake but I balance my pressure so that the wheels don't lock up. I use the brakes (*not* the engine) to slow the car down. Now, before I enter the corner, it is necessary to complete the downshift. For this corner I have gone down from fifth to fourth.

Because of the heavy braking, maximum traction is on the front tire contact patches, assuming that you haven't locked up the brakes. Remember to keep looking where you want to be going.

The Corner Turn-In Point

With the car going its slowest (almost 90mph), I reach my turn-in point, continue major braking (trailing the brakes), and turn into the corner, transferring the already forward-moving weight laterally, which "sets" the chassis—further compressing the springs and shocks and again increasing the tire contact patch. The left front (outside) tire now carries the majority of the adhesion for the steering and cornering.

I've used maximum braking while entering the corner but now begin to trail-brake, usually into the first third of the corner. Trail braking keeps the chassis set and maintains the downforce (or tire contact patch) while I aim for the apex area of the corner.

Remember, trail-braking is what happens after you have completed your major braking for a corner. Essentially, the moment you start turning into the corner you start decreasing the brake pressure, riding the brake into the first third of the corner, gradually releasing the pressure, and smoothly making the transition from brake to throttle, maintaining the balance of the car.

When setting up for a corner get your downshift completed during the major braking, just prior to turning in. That is, start your braking and, while braking, execute your heel-and-toe downshift from fifth to fourth. If the corner is so tight that you need to go down one more gear, just continue your downshift one more gear. (If you choose you can go directly form fifth to third, but just be sure you have slowed enough for a third gear turn.) If you complete your downshift too soon and let the clutch out before you should you may well over-rev the engine.

As soon as the downshift and major braking are simultaneously completed, the clutch pedal is smoothly released and *the right heel pivots back below the brake pedal*, which allows you to start easing pressure off the brake pedal ever so smoothly and gradually, finish the release at about the first third of the entry into the corner, then bringing up the throttle smoothly and heading for the apex area and the exit onto the straightaway.

As the car tracks into the first third of the corner, heading for the apex area, my right foot, slowly and precisely, starts to ease its way off the brake. All I'm doing by this time is dragging the brake pads on the rotor. The dragging pad keeps the chassis set. I'm not using this last stage of trail-braking to slow down; that was done as I first entered the corner with my major braking, then with the tire sidewalls scrubbing off some speed too.

In a low-speed corner you must be careful not to overbrake and lose your exit speed. If you do this, you are either braking too early, too long, too hard or a combination of all three.

In a higher-speed corner, one way to

tell when I've reached the limit of trail-braking is when the back end of the car starts to become a little light and just begins to slide out. When it reaches that point, I smoothly come all the way off the brake and start to squeeze the throttle on, transferring the weight smoothly to the rear tires. I do this in two distinctly separate motions. Don't just slide your foot from the brake to the throttle. Move it positively and smoothly.

The first third of the corner is nearing completion as the throttle is being eased on and I'm looking toward the apex area. The balance of throttle is important at this point. I feed in as much throttle as the rear wheels will take (smoothly). If the rear wheels start to lose traction, I ease halfway off the throttle a bit to recover the adhesion. If I take my foot all the way off the throttle and/or do it too abruptly, I lose my chassis set and tire contact patches, and the car goes into a skid.

The Corner Apex

Passing through the second third of the corner, the apex area, the car is now in its most stable condition during the corner, until after the exit onto the straightaway. The car is now under complete throttle control and all four tire patches are working for me. My steering is set for the exit and I have started to look for the exit point. If I did the first two thirds right, my exit should be perfect and I will be able to carry my speed down the entire straightaway.

My line through the corner has been set and I am committed. Too much gas

---

Any given corner can be broken up into three segments: entry, apex, and exit.

Parking lot autocross or gymkhana events can teach you a lot about controlling your car. Here I am following a student through a similar setup at my old Orange County facility in our original Datsun school cars. *Petersen Publishing*

will cause too much weight to come off the front tires causing me to lose front tire adhesion and cause the car to push or understeer. The weight transfer is being *gradually* moved to the rear of the car during acceleration. I ease on to the gas to maintain the forward stability and the suspension set.

As I feed in more throttle I am increasing the rear tire contact patches while at the same time adjusting the weight transfer from the outside front to the outside rear of the car. My acceleration is picked up more now and is smoothly increased to full throttle heading for the exit of the corner. Continually, I am focusing my eyes, not just where I am, but *where I want to go*.

To backtrack just a bit (just in case you forgot the term), exactly what is the *apex area* I keep referring to? Most books just call it "apex" or "clipping point." This, however, is a little bit of a misrepresentation. True, there is a geometric apex of a corner that is right in the middle of the turn. And the clipping point is where your inside front wheel physically is closest to the inside edge of the corner.

What you need to learn about is the driving *apex area*. I say apex *area* because, unlike the *geometric apex* the *apex area* varies in length. Every freeway off ramp, mountain curve, racetrack corner, or highway turn has an apex area. Some even have two. But every corner has at least one.

The variable factor in an apex area is the speed at which you arrive at the apex area combined with the length (or radius) of the curve. If for example, you have a 90degree corner, say on the street, you might have a short apex area. But on a high-speed corner on a race course, you could have an apex area five or six car

lengths or more. It really depends on the speed potential of the given corner.

Slow or fast, street or track, you want to hit the apex area properly to get maximum traction, stability, and acceleration out of the corner. The apex area is the part of the corner where your car is in its most stable condition and your tires are the closest to the inside edge of the corner. A longer apex area is necessary when driving or racing in the rain. Let's get back to the 90mph right-hand turn.

I am now feeding in full throttle and the centrifugal force is pushing my car to the outside edge of the corner. I have full traction for acceleration and I'm heading toward my chosen exit point. The apex area that I chose was about two-thirds of the way around the corner. My turn-in point to the corner was deeper and later than if I would have had a mid-corner apex area. By having a relatively late apex area, I have ensured that I will be on full throttle a little earlier and when I am on full throttle, the g forces acting on the car will not push it too far to the outside and off the road at the corner's exit. The car is heading pretty much in a straight line as I approach and exit the apex area.

The Corner Exit

This last third of the corner, the exit, is the easiest part if I did everything preceding it correctly; if I didn't it will become the most difficult.

I take care to feed in the throttle smoothly and evenly carefully avoiding wheelspin. Remember, you always want to exit long and wide in pretty much as straight a line as possible, in order to dissipate the unsettling forces that pick up momentum when the speed increases.

I have chosen a long and wide exit using all of the road possible. I will be easing out the steering, and feeding in the throttle smoothly, as I aim in a straight line for the exit point. Under full throttle, my car is just on the border of maximum traction and I am now in just a slight four-wheel drift—almost to the exit point. As I arrive at my exit point, I am already looking down the straightaway for the next corner.

If you're practicing this corner and your turn-in point was correct, you hit the proper apex area for your speed and your car, then you should still be on the correct line to be able to use the maximum road available at the exit. If you did everything right you were definitely faster than you were before you began using these techniques. You have left your old driving habits behind and now you drive a lot smoother with much more control.

In racing, remember that the earlier you can ease into full throttle in a corner, the quicker you will enter the straightaway. The quicker you enter the straightaway the sooner you will reach maximum speed. The sooner you reach maximum speed using the all-important *apex area* the quicker you get to the next corner. If you can reach full speed thirty yards earlier, you can carry that speed for the entire distance of the straightaway. On just one corner you might gain two or three tenths of a second. It really adds up. Add that little bit from one corner plus nine or ten more corners and, surprise, you've knocked a couple of seconds off your lap time.

Think of it this way: all the corners do is tie the straightaways together. The quicker you can exit a corner, the quicker you can get down the straightaway and to the next corner. The quicker you can move down the straightaways the quicker you can get to the finish. Get the picture!

But if you enter the apex area too early or don't hold the car in long enough, the slower you'll be, the more work you will be doing and the worse results you'll have. So think, figure out your corners, do them right, be smooth, and you'll be quick!

Just don't forget to set up and enter the corner properly to be able to have a quicker exit. On the street you will want to approach the corner the same basic way except to make a more shallow entry. And remember, the street apex areas are usually at least twice as long because your speeds are so much slower. Also the roads or lanes are usually much narrower than a racetrack, minimizing the amount of road you have available to use. On the street you really should be keeping your speeds down anyway. But, if you get that urge, you had better be smooth and precise, have a good check in your mirrors, know the area well, and make sure you don't cause someone else, who doesn't have your abilities, to have an accident. Most of all use your head and be careful, if not for yourself, for the others on the road. Remember, there is usually a run-off area on a racetrack but there are none on the street.

Choosing Gears and Downshifting

When downshifting, you must choose whether you need to go from fifth to fourth to third or directly from fifth to third—it all depends on the situation.

One of the most important factors to consider is that you make absolutely sure you have the proper rpm when you release the clutch if you've skipped one gear in your downshift. If you go through all of the gears you shouldn't have that problem, but it's easy to have too many revs if you come down, say fifth to third or

A composite of a corner. The numbers on the photo indicate the following actions: 1, under full braking. 2, start heel-and-toe downshift. 3, complete downshift. 4, start trail-braking. 5, complete trail-braking. 6, begin acceleration. 7, under full acceleration. 8, exit point. 9-10, this is the apex area. To put all of this in perspective, this section can be approximately six to seven seconds in a Formula Ford.

The proper entry and exit of a typical 90-degree corner. Note the long apex area is almost six or seven car lengths. A proper late apex area allows you to set up easily for the next corner.

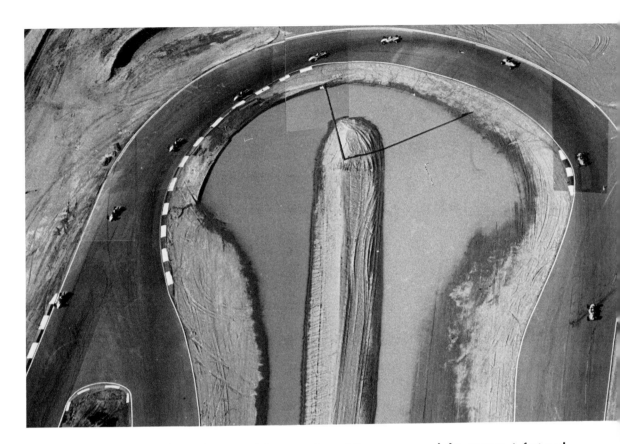

A long hairpin exiting and entering a straight-away. Note how deep into the turn before turn-in, then the apex area about three-quar-ters of the way around the corner. A fast and easy long exit. No problems.

The same turn as before but here I turned in too soon, entered too fast too early, apexed way too soon so the car drifted out too soon—the centrifugal force of cornering pushed the car to the outside and off course. If I had trail-braked to the middle of the turn I could have forced the car to stay inside and it could have been brought back to the prop-

er exit line—slower, but safer than running off the road. This entry, if executed properly, could become a passing line but you have to get the exit right.

Think of it this way: all the corners do is tie the straightaways together. The quicker you can exit a corner, the quicker you can get down the straightaway and to the next corner. The quicker you can move down the straightaways the quicker you can get to the finish.

fourth to second without using the gear in between. It is a bit faster, but you must be careful to save your equipment. An over-rev on a downshift is usually what breaks engines. No rev-limiter in the world can help your engine when that happens.

The nature of the race course can also make the decision for you. There's a bit more margin and safety if, for example, you use all the gears if you have a wall at the edge of the track or no run-off area. If you have lots of run-off area or the barriers are set well back from the track surface then, sure, go ahead and go directly into the lower gear.

One thing I might do (if I'm really going in deep, when I'm shifting from fourth directly to second) is just pass through third gear, and if I feel that my braking is

OK then I'll skip third and go on to second. It just gives a little more margin for error if the braking isn't quite sufficient. I could use third too, to put a little more weight transfer on the rear tires to help slow me some before second gear.

Early, Middle, and Late Apexes

When it comes to apex areas, there are early, middle, and late apex areas. Each corner is slightly different, but as a rule, the apex area on the racetrack is usually about two-thirds of the way around the corner. On the street, it will start in the middle and exit all the way around the corner.

The way to tell if you chose the right apex or not is quite simple. If you set up for the corner and come out of it having to add more steering to keep from running off the road, then you had too early an apex. Or perhaps, you hit the right apex but let the car drift out of the apex area too soon. The same thing happens: you end up with not enough road. Your front tires will have to be turned to correct for your mistake and it will slow you down.

If you've picked too late of an apex, then you most likely have slowed the car down much more than was necessary, and your car will be in way too tight. With a late apex, you will not be able to keep the speed up enough to drift the car out to the edge, to take full advantage of all of the road. This is safer and OK for the street, but decidedly slower on the racetrack.

Ideally, you want to come out of the corner long and wide. If you are coming from a narrow road to a wider one, you will have an earlier apex area because you will have more road to use when you exit the corner.

Just the opposite situation occurs

when you come from a wide road to a narrow one: you will have a late and long apex area.

Find a safe place to experiment and practice. Start slow and build up speed as you can handle it. Find out what happens if you apex early, late, or properly—but do it where you won't damage your car if you go off the road. And more importantly, where you won't hurt anyone else. That is one of the most important priorities of high-performance driving. It is a responsibility. Use your head and good common sense. A good place to practice these basics is to enter some local autocrosses.

At racing speeds it is important to hit the proper apex areas. If you don't, you'll find yourself slow—or off the road.

I remember one time while I was tire testing for Goodyear. I was at Daytona in a Cobra and it was early morning. The car was warmed up but I wasn't.

With the Cobra, it first understeers badly, then it goes into oversteer as the power is applied, then it reaches a nice, smooth four-wheel drift. It feels great once you get the hang of it. But this particular time, I was into the turn a little too fast, didn't turn in quite as soon as I should have (didn't warm the tires up properly either), and all of a sudden I found myself sideways. Embarrassing! Right in front of all the Goodyear people, the first lap of the first day of a week's worth of testing.

I spun. God, did I spin! I went for a hell of a ride. I did two 360s off onto the grass. I hadn't set up right for the apex, so the centrifugal force took over and pushed me right off the track. I slid to a stop, put it in the proper gear, and got going again. Simple as that. Had I been a little sharper, I would have turned in a little earlier, eased back on the throttle a little, and saved it—and saved a lot of embarrassment.

Controlling Oversteer for Drifts

That brings us to drifting, oversteer, and understeer. In a properly balanced car, properly set up, the optimum handling characteristic is neutral. For these examples we are assuming a neutral-handling car.

Drifting through a corner means that all four wheels are sliding through the turn

Four-wheel drifts are lots of fun as witnessed here with one of my students in one of our Ford Mustang school cars. Like I said, use your head about when and where to take your car to the limit— and keep the safety of others in mind when you practice.

with the desired throttle control, making it nice and smooth. In this condition you are at the "limit," just a fraction past the point of maximum traction, but in balance and in control. If the car is oversteering, the rear wheels are starting to slide. In understeer, the front wheels are starting to slide and the car won't go where you steer it.

You control the oversteer and understeer with the throttle and the steering, creating what is known as a four-wheel drift. Getting into a four-wheel drift is a lot of fun.

You can have power oversteer or simple oversteer. Power oversteer is when you come into a corner, set up trail-braking, and let the rear end slide out a little as you feed the throttle in, controlling it by the amount of throttle you feed in. Too much throttle and your power oversteer turns into simple oversteer and a spin-out.

Simple oversteer is a situation that usually indicates you're in trouble. You come into a corner braking too late, turn into the apex area with the front wheels sticking OK but the rear end is too light and you might lock up one or both of the rear tires. With all of the weight transfer on the front tire contact patches, the rear end might want to come around. More often, when you don't keep enough throttle on while heel-and-toe downshifting (sometimes even too much throttle), you'll momentarily lock up both rear wheels and go into a slide.

Sometimes you can still save it by easing in a bit of throttle, which transfers weight back to the rear wheels. Not a lot or the corner is history! That's not a lot of fun.

If you are in a power oversteer situation and come off the throttle too quickly, the rear end of the car will be gone. It will come around on you so quickly you won't have time to correct it with the steering.

Practice different lines. Heavy traffic or other situations will often prevent you from being able to drive the ideal line through a corner. George Follmer (16) and I (93) are on the right line for this corner at Riverside with a late-apex area. *Dave Friedman*

Controlling Understeer

Understeer (pushing or a front-wheel slide) is a situation in which you either turned in too early, at too high a rate of speed, in too high a gear, or got on the throttle too soon or to hard. If the later was the case, too much weight transferred *off* the front tire contact patches and they lost adhesion so the car wants to push you out of the corner.

If you turn into the corner a bit too early, hit too early an apex area and are going too fast, the car is being pushed to the outside of the corner by inertia. You want to get the car into the proper apex area or you will run out of road at the exit. You add steering but you car is still heading to the outside. You are under throttle but the gear you are in doesn't have sufficient torque to bring the rear end around enough to get you pointed right—the front wheels are still sliding.

Here's what you do: Ease off the throttle as this will lighten the rear wheels and transfer some of the weight back to the front tires, *the deflection of the sidewalls will scrub off some of your speed* and give you back your steering. The rear end will come around now, changing the angle of the car. Correct as much as you need with the steering and ease back into the throttle. The car will stabilize again but you lost your speed advantage out of the corner because you had to get off of the throttle due to a miscalculation. Downshift and get going.

Choosing a Line Through a Corner

In a warm-up session, before the race ever starts, I will try different lines through different corners to see what will happen if I have to go there during the race. I want to have possibilities available to me, before I have to do it out of necessity. I want to know if I can pass someone on the inside or the outside, going into or coming out of a given corner. I want to know if I can go high or low in a corner if there is someone spinning ahead of me. I want to know where I can go safely if I need to. That's just another aspect of knowing yourself, your car, and the road around you.

Experiment, find out what happens if you turn in too early, too late, or too deep. Find out what makes each apex area work in any kind of corner for you and your car. Find out in which types of corners your car works best and which kind of corners it doesn't work so well. The kinds of corners are unlimited—increasing radius, decreasing radius, negative camber, positive camber, banked, hairpin, high-speed—each is different.

Every corner you approach will be different. There is no miracle formula that will teach you one standard way for every corner. The procedure, yes, but the line and the apex area, no. It depends on you, your speed, your car, and how your car is prepared.

At the Grand Prix of Belgium at Spa several years ago, a novice Formula 1 driver remarked how he had difficulty doing a particular high-speed corner flat out in his Formula Ford; in his Formula 1 car, flat out (about 70mph faster) it was easy.

To learn to mathematically calculate your corners, I strongly recommend that you read Taruffi's book *The Technique of Motor Racing*. Use his calculations as a base. Then use your head and work it out from there.

On paper, corners can look simple and easy. The little figure in the drawings always makes it around the corner whether the diagram is correct or not. The photographs in this chapter of cars actual-

Every corner has an entry, apex area, and exit. Here I am discussing the proper cornering technique with students after an on-track session.

ly going through corners under power and g force loading gives you some real examples; but remember, your speed and your car (plus the amount of tire contact patch) and the way it is prepared will cause it to be slightly different. What we are giving you are the basics; the rest you'll have to find out from practice and experience.

If you do find yourself getting into some trouble (almost everyone does sooner or later), then we're about to tell you how to (we hope) get out of it, or at least make it less of a problem.

What I didn't count on was, after he hit the guardrail he shot right back across the track, right in front of me. Some choice I had: I could run right over the top of him or put my car sideways and spin myself. I threw my car sideways and hit him wheel to wheel. That was the end of my right rear suspension...broken. And, for both of us it was the end of the race,

on our last lap. Peter went by us as we were climbing out of our cars and won the race.

I should have used my head more. It was a two heat race but because I was so determined to beat Roy Pike, I didn't make it to the second heat.

When I crashed, the first thing I saw when I got out of my car was Fangio—Juan Manuel Fangio, the only five-time World Driving Champion. I had met him the day before and he had invited me to race in the Temporado Series in Argentina, strictly an invitational series of races. And, here I was, crashed right in front of him. He was sitting on the veranda of the Hotel du Paris. I thought to myself, "Oh, my God, how embarrassing." That was the end of Monaco for me for that year.

That kind of thing can happen easily to anyone in a racing situation but it is unnecessary and expensive. In racing, once you've committed to a decision there's usually no second chance. Experience will help you to make the right decisions but getting that little bit of experience can at times be costly. You must be sharp, alert, and quick with the proper decisions. A moment's lapse of concentration and away you go.

Most out-of-control situations are a result of lack of concentration, trying to go too fast too soon, or simple carelessness. Sure, just doing something wrong because you don't know better happens too, but usually it's from driving over your head. Above you or your car's ability.

If you're about to get into a situation that's going to be more demanding than you can handle, get out of it before you get into trouble. Listen to that little voice in your head that is trying to tell you to use your common sense. As your driving ability and experience become more refined, you will be able to read a situation before it happens (in most cases).

In the situation at Monaco, it was my first single-seater drive and the information that I was acting on was from Corvettes and Cobras. I didn't realize that when a single-seater with open wheels hits a guardrail, the car gets shot right back into the way. Full-fendered cars usually stay against the wall longer.

Most accidents and spins come from doing something wrong—or doing nothing at all—rather than making a wrong decision of where to go. Most of the time, a spin or an accident can be avoided if you know what to do, which takes practice and learned experience. One of the most important rules to remember in an emergency situation; always look where you want to go, not where you are.

Avoiding Skids, Slides, and Spins

Now comes the hard part. Skid, slide, spin all mean the same thing, you are out of control; or almost. We'll try to give you some control over those problems instead of just being a passenger and watching it all happen around you.

One of the first things that you probably were told when you started driving was that if the rear end of the car starts to slide out or skid, turn your steering wheel in the direction the car is sliding. That's right; it works! How well it works is up to you. Your reactions have to be fast—lightning fast!

Again, you have to be in fine tune with your car and know as soon as the skid starts to happen how much, how fast, and when to correct. The main thing is, quickly, as fast as you can, *move that steering wheel!* Immediately turn it in the same direction the rear end is starting to slide so you can start to stabilize the slide. If you react too slowly, turn the wheel too slowly, or not far enough soon enough, you still will probably spin out.

Getting to Know Trouble

No one wants to get into trouble but if you put many miles on a car, racing or on the street, you will inevitably be confronted by an emergency situation. This is where all that you have learned and trained for will come into play. You'll have to make a decision...and quick! Your reactions will have to be lightening fast. Your judgment will have to be correct. You will only have a split second to do everything! It better be right.

Basically there are two types of emergency situations: one that originates with you or your car and the other that is a result of someone else's actions. The most common is one that occurs from you or your car, usually because you become careless or sloppy—not just in your driving but also in your car's upkeep and preparation. Maybe you lose a wheel, the throttle sticks open or the brakes fail...you know, the usual things that can go wrong. There are a lot of things that can go wrong when you are driving. So, as I said before, do the best you can to maintain your car properly.

If you do that, then the only thing you'll have to worry about is yourself...and the other guy who maybe doesn't care as much for his car or his driving technique.

Avoiding Trouble on the Racetrack

If you are racing make sure that you try various lines in the corners to give yourself an option if something happens in front of you.

At Monaco in 1965, I was driving a Cooper Formula 3 car for Ken Tyrrell that Jackie Stewart campaigned the year before. I had set the fastest qualifying lap and was running well in the race. I was just taking second place from Peter Revson. Monaco is really a tight circuit, even for a Formula 3 car. To squeeze both of us through a turn I had to use a bit of the road...and a bit more. I had two wheels on the pavement and the other two on top of the hay bales at the edge of the circuit.

I passed Peter and was so scared that I didn't move the steering wheel or make any correction on the throttle. If I did I would go over the bales and into the harbor. I didn't feel like going for a swim. So I smoothly and gently kept my steering and throttle just where they were and eased the car back down onto the road again. I completed my pass as I was coming down off the hay bales and into Tabac corner.

After I got by Peter, I had Roy Pike, the race leader, in my sights and decided I was going to catch him. There were only about six or eight laps left in the race, and I finally caught up to him and pressed him as hard as I could. He started driving harder and I was driving harder, too. For me to catch him meant that I was obviously faster. If you are in the lead and all of a sudden there is someone out of nowhere on your tail you know he is a lot faster; so that really makes you try harder. In Roy's case, even though he was leading, the harder he drove the slower he went.... Remember, smoother is quicker.

I wanted that lead. I had two spots picked out to pass him. One was out of the tunnel and the other was out of the Casino bend. As we headed up the hill to the Casino, I was about two feet behind him and I went deeper into the corner—as deep as I could, even over my head. He went in even deeper and I knew he wasn't going to make it. He didn't. He started to spin into the guardrail and I dove underneath him. See p 104

There is a way out! If you get into a slide and don't correct it either soon enough or quick enough, simply turn the wheel back straight, front wheels pointing straight ahead. Put the clutch in (or shift into neutral with an automatic). The car will do a 180degree spin and come out straight going down the road backward. *Gently* squeeze on the brakes, coming to a stop. Don't worry about the other peo-

ple; believe me, they are watching out for you!

There are a lot of different things that will make a surface slippery or slicker than normal: rain, snow, ice, or other weather conditions, oil, gas, sand, gravel—with each you will lose traction. The tires don't have enough adhesion and the car slides.

The most common skid that you will be confronted with is when the rear end of the car slides out on you. Left or right, it's the same. Usually it has happened as a result of going into a corner too fast, or incorrectly, or hitting a slick area causing your rear wheels to oversteer. This can happen also from not adding enough throttle on a heel-and-toe downshift causing the rear wheels to lock up; or putting on too much throttle in a corner before the direction and set of the car can handle it; or jumping on the brakes too hard, locking up the rear wheels. Whatever the cause, here's what to do to correct it.

Stay off the brakes! If you don't you might lose your steering and make it even worse. Then, *quickly*, steer in the direction that the rear of the car is sliding. If you have full throttle on, ease off enough to bring traction back to your rear wheels. Don't pull all the way off of the throttle or it will take what weight you have on the rear wheels and transfer it forward, making the rear end even lighter.

In wet weather ease *all the way* off the throttle to lessen the skid or slide. If you caught the first slide, be ready for one in the other direction (caused by over-correcting). If it happens, adjust for the slide in the other direction. This is a quick situation, and can happen back and forth several different times. Be ready each time and keep the car going in a forward motion or direction. Correct each skid by turning into the direction the back end is sliding, *as fast as you can.*

If the front end of the car is skidding in understeer, the correction to keep you from going off the road is simple but be careful because you'll find oversteer when you come out of an understeer condition.

If the front end is pushing to the outside you will have to ease off the throttle to transfer the weight back to the front tires to gain steering control. The rear of the car should get lighter and your steering will come back; but the rear may then want to move out, so get ready to correct the steering in the same direction the rear end is sliding. If you can't correct your rear-wheel slide you will end up going the wrong way.

Remember to look in the direction you want to go, as quickly as possible and you will end up going in that direction. When the slide is corrected, straighten your steering wheel, fast! You easily know where straight ahead is because you al-ways grab your steering wheel at 3:00 and 9:00 so when your hands are there you should be going straight ahead.

When you make corrections in a skid make them quick and positive. Keep your car going in that direction. If you are racing it makes a lot of difference in lap times, so try not to skid. Every time you have to correct in a major fashion, you are losing time. Being consistent and smooth saves time.

What if your car reaches an angle of 90degrees or more to the direction you were traveling and it looks like you won't be able to catch the slide? Don't worry yet—you can, hopefully, still save the car, but the fast lap is now history. Again, *stay off the brakes!* What you want to do now is spin the car the rest of the way around and create a forward-180. This is where you are now traveling in the same direction as before but backward. Remember, the faster you are traveling the bigger the spin is going to be, and the faster you will have to correct it.

Notice, you turn the wheels in the direction of the skid. Along about this time you need to really have a fine touch on the throttle to keep it from coming on around. I can't emphasize enough the need for fast reactions. I saved this one but it was almost to the point of no return. Notice how my head, although looking where I want to go, is only slightly tilted, keeping full body contact with the seat.

As soon as the car gets past 90degrees (it's too late to keep it from spinning), straighten the wheel, put the clutch in, and put the car in neutral. If you don't keep the clutch in or put the car in neutral, the drive wheels will push against the directional movement of the car. That's a good way to flat-spot your tires, stall your engine and get into even more trouble.

You are still going in the same direction you originally were, but now you're backward (a 180degree spin). At this point, there are two things you can do. One, carefully drive (back up) the car to a safe place to stop it; or two, spin it back around (if you have sufficient speed) and get going in the direction you had planned to go originally (a reverse 180degree spin).

If you've still got sufficient speed while heading backward and have enough room to negotiate, without endangering someone else, then it's time to execute a reverse 180degree spin. This is where you start out backward and end up going forward. It's not that difficult if you stay off the brakes. If you don't, you won't have enough speed to execute the maneuver.

So, here you are, heading backward at over 70mph. What to do? While looking in your mirrors to see where you want to go, give the steering wheel a good crank, as fast as you can, snap-spin the steering wheel as fast as you can toward the object you want to miss (clutch in, no brakes) to a complete full-lock position. Turning the wheel either direction will work. If there is a wall or barrier on one side of you steer that direction, since you're heading backward you'll spin in the other direction. The same as with the forward-180, when the car gets past 90degrees, straighten the wheel...you know, 3:00 and 9:00. When

you straighten the wheel to go straight again it *must* be done fast and firmly.

Don't forget that during the whole procedure, the clutch is in and/or the car is in neutral, and the engine is kept running. While the car is coming around to straight ahead again, keep the clutch in but shift it into the gear that's going to handle the speed of your exit. That means you'll have to have your revs matched for your next exit speed just like a normal downshift. As soon as you're heading in the right direction again ease out the clutch, ease on the throttle, and away you go.

To do a 360degree spin, you just combine a forward-180 and a reverse-180 and you'll be heading in the right direction if you're fast enough and do it right. World champion Keke Rosberg accomplished this at the Long Beach Grand Prix one time when he spun going for the lead—and only lost one position. It works! It just takes practice...like everything else. The best place to learn is on a skid pad. There you won't hurt yourself, your car or anyone else.

At my school, skid control training is an important part of the overall program and is found in each of my driving courses. We use specially designed skid control cars that can simulate any given emergency skid condition. The next step after skid control is accident avoidance.

Avoiding Accidents

The most important thing to understand is that you can't stop as fast as you can avoid, even with anti-lock brakes (ABS). This is especially true at racing speeds.

In my first sports car race, driving my Morgan Plus 4 at Santa Barbara in 1956, I was coming into Turn Nine at the old airport course and some guy in a Mercedes 300SL Gullwing lost it right in front of me. First race...great! Right in front of me. I swerved to miss him and ended up spinning myself. Everyone said, "Oh, wow, you did great; a great job spinning to miss that guy." The fact of the matter was I really didn't try to spin, all I wanted to do was miss him. Well, I missed him.

That was my first incident in a race. There have been many more but through experience I learned how to avoid a problem, usually without having to spin to avoid it. On many occasions I've had to swerve to miss other people spinning, or to miss oil dropped from a blown engine, or whatever.

It can be done safely and usually without incident if you are really *alert*, if you're *looking far enough ahead* and if your *reactions are quick enough*. Here we are again, right back to concentration, alertness, anticipation, and reaction speed—everything that you need and have if you are physically and mentally fit.

Avoidance is usually quite easy. Someone spinning in front of you is a typical situation on a race circuit. On the street it may be a car door opening, a child chasing his or her ball, or a dog running in front of you that must be avoided.

First, *don't use your brakes.* Come off the throttle, immediately! This transfers the car's weight and momentum forward giving you a larger tire contact patch. Second, steer to avoid the object. Usually, aim for where it has been—not the direction it is going. At speed, a slight turn of the wheel is enough, then immediately correct to your straight ahead direction (3:00 and 9:00 on the wheel) and feed back in the throttle. This now transfers the weight back to your rear tires, giving you straight-line traction.

Object past. Where to steer to? It depends on what you are avoiding, but in the case of a spinning race car the best place to head for is where it has already been. That's to say if the car in front of you spun to the left and hit the wall it will go to the right in front of you; so head where the car has already been, to the left.

In a real high-speed situation you'll have to be faster than you can imagine. And you'll have to be perfect. If you stay off the throttle too long in an avoidance maneuver, the rear end will get light and you can spin too. Therefore it's really important to get the power back on (smoothly) as soon as you can see that you are going to miss what's in front of you.

If you can't avoid the object and you are forced to stop, make sure your steering wheel is turned straight ahead. Get ready...we are about to stop...fast...Panic City! If there's no place to go and it's either stop or crash then you'd better know how to stop: cadence brake. Nice word? Nice procedure. It is the only thing that might stop you. And there is no guarantee, it depends on how fast you are going, how much distance you have in which to stop, and how well you cadence brake.

Cadence Braking

The cadence braking procedure works well especially in wet weather, but it works in the dry too. Your foot comes off the gas, weight transfers to the front, increasing the tire contact patches. If you ease on the brakes like in a normal braking situation you simply won't have time to stop. If you panic and lock-up your brakes, you've just lost your steering and you'll slide right into what you're trying to avoid. Using cadence braking you'll stop in half of distance of normal.

During training at the school, each maneuver is explained in detail, then demonstrated, before the student tries it. The same thing goes for a forward 180, reverse 180, and the combination of the two. We teach you from behind the wheel how to handle your car in these situations.

Here's how it goes: Put the brakes on full, just to the locking point, then rapidly come clear off of them, then on again full, then off again full, on, off, on, off rapidly. The faster you pump them on and off, the faster the car will stop.

It takes some practice but it works, if you do it fast enough. Pump them as fast as you can on and off till the car comes to a stop. Those cars equipped with an ABS braking system do this for you, except electronically, all the time. ABS is a great braking system and in most situations on most cars is a wonderful option.

Maybe you don't want to come to a complete stop or maybe you want to change direction as you're slowing down. Here's how: You must be able to keep your steering ability. Come completely off the brakes for an instant, make your steering correction, and continue your cadence braking until stopped or slowed sufficiently to avoid the problem. If, for some reason, you are in a full locked braking situation (which you shouldn't be but you are) and you must change your direction slightly (say if you're on ice), come off the brake, make your steering adjustment, and then cadence brake—don't just hold the pedal to the floor.

The key is to feel everything your car is doing and anticipate what might happen because when it does you aren't going to have much time to make more than one decision. Practice, practice, practice.... Find somewhere safe like a vacant parking lot and see what your car does.

OK, here's what you've been waiting for: a plug for my school. It takes practice on a skid pad to find out what it really takes to cadence brake, correct massive oversteer, spin 180 and 360degrees and the like, safely. My school has a fantastic skid-control instruction. Most of the other schools don't. Some don't think that it's necessary, others just don't have the facilities or the room that is required. It is, however, a really important step in learning complete car control. You have to know exactly what you and your car will do when the situation presents itself. And it will, sooner or later.

At my new, state-of-the-art facility near Phoenix, Arizona, I dedicated a large area of the facility to skid control. I have six highly advanced and dedicated skid cars for student instruction; three rear-wheel-drive Ford Mustangs and three front-wheel-drive Ford Tauruses.

Driving in Bad Weather

Adverse weather conditions present even greater hazards and the need for even greater smoothness and concentration.

In the rain, a typical turn can be transformed into an instant nightmare if overdone. Your line through a turn in the rain will start a little sooner and slower for a shallow entry. Your apex area might be twice as long and lower or higher on the road than your normal racing line because in the rain that's where the traction is.

You have to judge the shape and type of turn and you'd better get it right. Where the rubber has been placed on the track will become more slippery than where there is no rubber. So, where you have the greatest traction in the dry, from rubber build-up, the opposite can happen in the rain.

You want to have a slightly higher, more stable and smoother line. You may even have to straddle the rubber that has been laid down, sometimes higher or lower because of puddles. Question: Why? Answer: Maximum traction!

You now know that everything you do in a car must be smooth. When braking or accelerating, it must be eased into and out of. In rain or other adverse conditions you can multiply that by about five times. If you aren't smooth, you are off the road. When you drive in adverse weather you must be even more alert, and every little

thing that you do must be extra smooth, gentle, and precise. You must be going decidedly slower in the rain or you'll be off the road.

Driving in Traffic

Good anticipation comes from experience and learning to watch the other people you're coming up on, then get familiar with them. Not just on the racetrack or driving but get to know them personally too. You need to get to know their personality traits that can help you on the circuit. Experience is learning to read other people too. Learning their moves and seeing what they do and how they handle themselves in a variety of situations.

The same goes for traffic, passing and drafting. Look far enough ahead to judge and get to know your competition, keep alert, and anticipate. With experience you should be able to take it all in and make the correct decisions.

Each circumstance is different—but learn from watching. Just because the driver in front of you gets the passing flag, don't expect him to pull over and let you by. It completely depends on that driver, so you may get plenty of room or you may have to race him to get past. Just remember, a clean pass is the responsibility of the overtaking driver, not the driver being passed.

That's where experience and how well you learned to read the competition come in handy. The driver might make it look like you are getting a lot of room then slam the door on you. An epic battle between Alain Prost and Ayrton Senna for the World Championship in 1989 saw the season title decided in Japan by just a maneuver. Prost opened the door for his McLaren teammate, Senna, and took him out. Prost was World Champion and Sen-

Skid Control, an essential part of the total high-performance program. I use it in the Executive Protection and Law Enforcement Academy programs, too. It's amazing what you can learn on a skid pad about the car and yourself.

na Vice-Champion. Just keep alert and watch everybody. It's a lot better to profit from someone else's mistake than from your own (Sandro Nannini won the race for Benetton Ford).

Traffic and passing are nothing more than mental gymnastics. Everyone is trying to psych out the other driver. The one who doesn't get psyched is the one who will do well.

In drafting, you can pick up a draft of at least six or eight car lengths behind the car in front of you. A lot depends on how fast you are running, but generally the closer you get the easier it is to run faster. You are in what is referred to as the car's "slipstream." This makes both cars run faster than if there was only one car cutting through the air. But there are problems, too.

A good example of drafting can be seen at any NASCAR race with the leaders usually running nose to tail. They run faster but the second car, although it gets better fuel economy, it can really have a problem with cooling if they run too close too long. The lead car has a problem too, as the second car can easily whip out from behind and gain momentum in the clean air and easily pass the leader.

In many of the single-seater races now, especially with the highly advanced ground effects, it is extremely difficult to drive close to the car in front due to the extreme turbulence created by the ultrahigh down-force that is created. The turbulence can cause both the car in front and the car in the rear to become unstable. Know what your car will do in all conditions.

In traffic you need to have a plan to get through. You're going to have to make your plans and decisions quick, but once you do, you're committed so it better have been the right decision. After you get by one car forget about that one and start concentrating on the next...how you're going to get by and where...plan, think, and be quick and decisive. And watch what's happening...look for weakness and

One important thing you need to learn in racing is the ability to anticipate when someone in front of you may be getting into trouble—especially important when you are following a competitor closely. Stay alert, always! And look well ahead of you—and the other car—as well.

strengths—that goes for both the car and the driver. See what corner he or she is really having trouble with and work on them there. Try different lines yourself to see what you can do at that spot. When the other driver's really messed it up, go for it.

Going Off the Road

When you do go off the road (and you will sooner or later), the most important thing to do is to *turn the wheels straight* in that instant just before you leave the road. If you don't you'll dig a wheel in and probably flip over and roll.

I still compete in a lot of vintage racing events, driving beautiful, fast, and expensive old race cars. In a race not too long ago, we were running in a full but mixed field of mid-1960s racers. It was one of the last races of the day and the sun was getting low. About halfway through the race someone lost an engine on the main straight. Oil was everywhere.

The last corner was a flat-out top-gear corner leading onto the straight. Before an oil flag could come out three cars lost it. One spun down the middle of the track

and continued. One spun to the outside and crashed hard against the wall. The third almost saved it. The driver corrected just right, was scrubbing speed, and the car had stabilized. The car was still heading off the road, but at least it was moving with its front wheels first and would have had just a drive through the mud....

But the driver didn't straighten the wheels as the car left the road and the poor little TR-3 snapped into a violent roll. The driver was OK but the Triumph was really bent. the driver did everything right but straighten the wheels as the car left the road. Maybe no one ever told the driver to do that....

The next most important thing to do when you run off the road is *don't hit anything*.

Assuming that you don't have a problem with that, the next thing is to either get the car stopped or get back on the road. Let's say that you don't need to stop because all that happened was you apexed too early and you ran out of pavement at the exit, putting two wheels off the road. There is no real problem if the shoulder will support the car and the edge of the road is absolutely even, without a lip. Ease off the throttle smoothly and hold your line. Don't try to steer immediately back onto the pavement or you could dig in a wheel on the edge of the pavement and spin or roll the car while attempting to come back on the road. Look for a smooth and even bit where the road meets the off-road and try to get back on there.

Again, like most situations: *Stay off the brakes!* Hold your line, maintain your traction, and ease smoothly and carefully back onto the road surface.

The same thing goes for having all four wheels off course—ease back on where you can safely. If there is a grass surface at the edge of the road be prepared to quickly correct any oversteer that might follow and be ready to ease back on the throttle a little if your tires lose traction. But stay off the brakes!

Driving Front-Wheel-Drive Cars

Most cars on the road now are front-wheel-drive. For better or for worse, they are less costly to produce so we're stuck with them. The manufacturers have convinced us that they are better, but then what they really want, is to sell cars and if

it's cheaper to make them, then that's better too.

The above-mentioned procedures will work with almost all cars except front-wheel-drive vehicles. With front-wheel-drive you have a lot more weight over the front wheels, increasing the tire contact patches, but a lot less weight at the rear and possibly a lot less traction at the rear too. Front-wheel-drive is great if you only want to drive in snow, but there are a lot of other road surfaces on which they are less than wonderful.

Cornering techniques as well as oversteer and understeer characteristics are slightly different with front-wheel-drive. Front-wheel-drive cars have a nasty characteristic called power understeer with the front wheels (the ones you have to steer with too). Interesting concept? And different.

You brake, enter a corner in the normal way, complete your downshift, and trail brake into the corner. You must ease off the brake or the inside rear wheel (probably almost off the ground by now) will lock and make the already light rear end want to swing around even more (remember, this is still oversteer). This puts an even greater load on your outside front

Rain causes the track surface to be especially slippery. With horsepower and handling of a 427 Cobra, you had to be forcefully gentle with a light touch and feel to control the car in the rain. *Motorsport*

wheel. If the rear starts to come around you must *accelerate* to *pull* yourself out of the corner. The acceleration transfers the weight again to the rear and increases the rear tire contact patch and thus the traction.

So far, so good, but if you put in too much throttle to save the back end you might lose the front. The car might go into understeer (or in this case, power understeer) and the front end will, with acceleration and even steering correction, push to the outside. Most of the car's weight is on the front and that oddly enough will be forcing the tires to lose adhesion. What you must do if the front end starts to go is *stay off the brakes!* In this case you have a throttle problem too.

If you come off the throttle all the way, both the front and the rear will lose traction and you'll be gone! If you stay on the throttle the front will completely wash out and you'll be gone! What to do? Cadence Throttle.

To cadence throttle, come off the throttle quickly, then depress it again just as quickly, on/off, on/off, just like cadence braking. This will get you through the turn, a bit jerky, but you'll make it through the corner.

Don't try to corner this way in each turn. It's not the fastest way and it'll tear up your car. If you break a CV joint you'll have to just park it (if you clip too many curbs you'll probably break one too). One more time, do it right and maximize traction. Cadence throttle...front-wheel-drive only. It can get you out of trouble.

Overcoming Fear

Maybe racing will scare you no matter what you are driving...one more reason to start out with something you can handle. If racing scares you too much, then you probably aren't going to make it past driving school, so you won't be looking for a car to buy. But if racing scares you just a little—join the crowd!

A typical front-wheel-drive car entering a corner(not trail-braking as there are no brakelights). Weight is shifted forward and to the outside front. Note the patch area of all tires in this situation.

There are times that anyone is going to be scared—out around the limit of traction for instance. If you are going to be successful then you are going to find out about *your* limits, your *car's* limits, and your *tires'* limits. When you do you will be over your head, you'll slide, you'll spin (maybe even crash), and you'll go right back for more.

Fearlessness won't get you any place but in the hospital, but combine that extra bit of daring with smoothness, consistency and precise control and you've just discovered that one more bit of necessary character that will make you a successful racing driver. If you aren't scaring yourself a bit at the limit then you are probably going too slow and aren't at the limit. By this time you might want to take one of my advanced racing courses where we evaluate you on a one-to-one basis and always get you going quicker and with more confidence.

10

Getting into Racing

Away we go into the never-never-land of buying a race car. Stop! Wait a minute! Is it really what you want? Ask yourself a few questions before you take that big and expensive step. Big question here? Do you really have what it takes? Time? Talent? Determination? And lots of money?

How do you know you are even going to like racing? Have you ever driven a car at its limit? Are you going to panic the first time you get sideways? Good possibility.

Let's put it this way: Do you want to spend $30,000 on a car that's going to scare you to death? Or, maybe driving around by yourself is OK but you nearly run off the road to get out of the way of someone trying to pass you. Don't like traffic? How do you find out till you try it? And, how do you try it without buying a car? Please read on.

High-Performance Driving Schools

One of the fastest and cheapest ways to learn if you like driving a car fast and to find out if you might make a good race driver is to take a high-performance driving or racing course at a nationally respected driving school. This first investment can either stop a career before it ever starts or get it headed in the right direction with a minimum of cost.

At this point don't waste your money on a race car. *Invest in yourself*. You'll have more to show for it. Racing is *not* like driving fast on the street. Not even close! It doesn't matter how closely you follow the sport or how sure you are that you want to race, until you try it you'll never really know what it's like. People can tell you what it's like but until you try it for yourself you'll never know. You may even surprise yourself and be better than you think.

Racing is expensive, there's a lot to learn, and it can be dangerous, so get the best training and as much experience you can before you ever think about buying a car. Attending driving schools is the least expensive way to learn how to drive a race car. It isn't a bad idea to do a couple of schools for the experience. Most have

Give yourself the best possible chance of becoming a successful race car driver: start out with the instruction offered by a professional driving school. Here Bobby Unser, Jr., and I are discussing driving techniques during an advanced instruction session.

advanced instruction too. And when it comes to doing the SCCA school for getting your license, do the whole thing, even though they waive the first weekend. The experience is what you will need. The more track time you can get the better.

Most schools will teach you the proper way to do things, on an individual basis, before you have a chance to learn the "traditional way" of doing them wrong. The traditional way, trial and error, can be costly and not gratifying. It causes a lot of potentially talented drivers to give up, fall by the wayside. Sometimes it's money, disappointment in the car they've bought, or just not being able to get around the track properly (which could be the car or the preparation too). Many people are lost without really giving themselves a fair chance.

Try a school first. Prepare *yourself* before you ever think about buying a race car or converting your street car to a racer; enroll in a school. It's also an ideal way of picking up advice and tips about starting racing. All of the instructors have

been or are active racers. Pick their brains.

It will take a lot more time and money to reach the same level of driving expertise by the trial and error method than by proper school training and instruction. Many trial and error drivers *never* reach the proficiency of the school graduate. Any racing school is better than none, but if you are really serious you might want to try a couple of different schools before you embark on that long and expensive road of race car ownership.

I feel that the Bob Bondurant School of High Performance Driving offers the most complete and thorough instruction. You want to be sure that you attend a school that will provide you with the firmest foundation possible. The Bondurant school is the only one that starts from a high-performance 5.0 liter Roush race-prepared V-8 Ford Mustang and progresses to single-seater Formula Ford race cars.

I believe that while learning, students must have an instructor riding with them (as we do at the Bondurant school) to see exactly what mistakes are made and get them corrected immediately. It is also necessary to ride with an instructor to see exactly what he or she does—not just what he or she might say. You'll see the proper use of hands on the wheel, good feet positions on the pedals, heel-and-toe downshifting, trail-braking, and proper seating position. From them you will learn to use your eyes better and look way ahead. To see the turn properly and what the road ahead is like, especially with other cars on it, are all important too. The proper use of your eyes in both racing and driving on the road everyday can save your life or keep you from having an accident. Plus, when racing, it can give you the quickest lap times, consistently.

From here, I do recommend that you, providing that you still want to race, try other schools as well. Many of the other schools are geared in the direction of Formula Ford. My school includes that as part of the total program, but by no means limits you to just that (some students just aren't comfortable in single-seaters).

The Bob Bondurant School of High Performance Driving now has a special program that actually puts you in competition with the other students, called the Bondurant Pro Driver Search (PROsearch). This program will take the top twenty-five students out of the 250 participants and find out which is quickest. The best of the competition wins a three-race drive in a Tom Gloy-prepared Trans-Am Mustang V-8. The runner-up wins one Trans-Am race in the same car.

Some of the other schools now sponsor racing series too. Any of these series provide you with a well-prepared car and actual racing competition time. Your investment is your time and a minimal amount of money—far less than it you had to buy a car and field it yourself. If after a few races you feel that this isn't quite what you wanted, you can just walk away. You won't have the worry of owning and preparing your own car (that probably didn't work right anyway) that you will have to get rid of, probably at a loss.

My school offers the most thorough instruction anywhere, with a ratio of three

To familiarize students with the circuit, they take their first laps behind an instructor. The instructors study the student's racing line through the various turns. As well as riding with the students in the Mustangs, the instructor follows the student, observing what the student is doing. After the session they stop and go over everything.

Students in my school start out in 5.0 liter V-8 Ford Mustang GTs then move to the faster and more responsive Formula Fords.

After you have mastered the Ford Mustangs you're moved up to the Formula Ford cars. Crawling into the narrow cockpit of one of these babies—you eyes are about level with tops of the tires—is a real thrill for most students. It's still even fun for me.

students to one instructor. Every student has his or her own car to drive throughout the program that is maintained by my own professional staff of mechanics. And, unlike many schools, we have plenty of spare and back-up cars should you have any problems. All of my instructors are personally trained by me and each are good competitors in their chosen classes of competition.

The instruction and its completeness vary a lot from school to school but you will get what you pay for. In some cases a lot more. How much you learn and how well you learn is up to first you, the school's basic curriculum, and then how good the instructor is. Any school is better than no school, but some are definitely going to teach you a lot more. It really all comes down to you. If you don't listen, don't follow instructions, and a lot of time it's easier not to, you are only cheating yourself.

Go to a driving school with the attitude that you are going to learn all that the instructors can possibly teach you, and you'll do well. It's not a vacation or going around the track in a parade—it's serious business. It's work and it will tire you out, but it can also be satisfying. It's one of the most self-satisfying, personally rewarding, learning experiences you'll ever have. I know, I see it every day!

Planning Your Racing Career

OK, let's assume that you've gone to a racing school, or better yet a couple of them, competed in a series, and decided that you want to be a road racer, or maybe an oval-track racer. Now what?

Yes, you might want to buy a car and go from there, but it is really advised to put together a whole plan and package, complete with schedule and goals. It's OK to set your goals high, after all it's all up to you and your talent (money helps a lot too). What you need first is a license: SCCA (Sports Car Club of America), IMSA (International Motor Sports Association), USAC (United States Automobile Club), NASCAR (National Association of Stock Car Auto Racing), or whatever you chose to compete in. What kind of racing do you want to do? How much money do you have to spend. Until you've done some racing and won some races you probably won't find a sponsor unless you own the company. So, guess who's going to foot the bills? Right. *You!* So, let's get the most for your money.

If you own your own company, you can write your racing off for PR, promotion, and advertising purposes if you carry the company name on the car. You can al-

so use the car as a company morale booster when you do well! Racing is a great vehicle to entertain special clients on a weekend outing.

Just because you don't have a car yet doesn't mean the you can't go to the licensing body's driving school. You might have a friend who will loan you his or her car or maybe you can rent one for the weekends of the school (still cheaper than buying). The most popular licensing schools are those of the SCCA. For information on all of the current requirements and fees you should contact the SAAC directly. They will be able to inform you as to when they are holding their schools and where within your region.

To get a novice license with the SCCA you must satisfactorily complete two weekends of SCCA drivers school or one private competition driving school (such as the Bob Bondurant School of High Performance Driving) and one weekend of the SCCA school. It is really recommended that even though they waive one of the school weekends, take it anyway. It is good inexpensive practice and it will both give you more track time and help to better familiarize you with their racing procedures. For full and current details you'd be wise to contact the club. Things change so keep current.

For an IMSA license, you are eligible for a provisional license after satisfactorily completing an approved competition school (like the Bondurant school). Again contact IMSA directly, or any other sanctioning/licensing body for the most current regulations on the racing series in which you are interested in competing.

You'll want to find out all of the rules and classes available in all of the sanctioning groups, so let's get the leg work started. I know, I know! You want to get to the good part...buying a car. Hold on. We're just about there. Don't forget, you are learning! So, listen, take a deep breath and hold on. Here we go!

Buying a Race Car

Time.... Take your time. There's not the rush that you think. We've already established that it's better to ease into things than jump into full throttle right away, so why would it be different with buying a race car? It's not. Chances are that you're going to have to wait for a school anyway. (SCCA schools are usually only once a year, just before the season starts). Make use of your time to observe. You probably have picked out a class or a series that either fits you pocketbook, your self image, or hopefully both.

Place your priorities where they belong; reliability, affordability, and competitiveness. Use your head, take your time and be sure of what you are getting. *Reliability is a must.* You have to be able to concentrate on your driving to do well, so make sure you buy a car that you aren't going to worry about keeping together. Both reliability and affordability are going to be determining factors in what you end up buying, but try to get something that will be competitive as you progress too.

Don't forget to add the necessary option to the program too: *common sense!* Forget about, at least for now, the high-priced formulas and the super-fast racers—they are not novice cars and they will *not* help you learn.

A superfast car is too dangerous for learning; it is usually unforgiving and expensive to boot. By superfast I mean Atlantic, Indy-Lights, Can-Am, GTP, Indy-Cars, you get the idea. These cars, for most, are out of the question from the affordability standpoint but some think they should start at the top if they have the money to do so. Forget it!

Start in a smaller, less-powerful car. Find out what you are doing with a car you can handle. You have to learn to set it up for different circuits. Keep it simple. You should have a great deal of respect for a race car but you shouldn't be afraid of it. Start out with a car that you can feel comfortable in and that you think you can master and explore your limits as well as you car's. Then you will be learning. Field a first-class effort in whatever class you can afford. It's better to have a first-class Showroom Stock car than a bare-boned Super-Vee with no spare parts. You can move into faster cars after you master the slower ones.

Maybe after attending a racing school you have decided that Formula Ford is the series for you. That's a good choice, especially if you have aspirations of becoming professional. It is an extremely competitive series, and in many regions there are pro race series too. Formula Ford is a popular series with a lot of talent in the ranks so you'll be in some quick and good company as well as really learning to race wheel-to-wheel.

Formula Fords are real race cars, they are fast without being ridiculous for the beginner, and they are both sophisticated and reasonably affordable. If you decide to go in that direction you will learn a lot about driving, racing, and chassis set-up.

The same can be said for sports racers, only they are full-fendered racing cars that look great, handle great, and have a little more power for better throttle control. And, they have more space to put your sponsors' logos!

If you have decided that you want to start out in one of the production categories, great! On the SCCA regional level there can be good competition and it is relatively inexpensive. Showroom Stock is the least expensive way to start and it is good experience. Improved Touring is also a great place to start.

One important word on this: If you are considering making your own street car into a race car, *forget it!* It is ridiculously expensive, time consuming, and probably one of the worst investments you can make at this point of your career. You will put lots more time and money into converting your car than if you buy one that is race-ready.

"Ready-to-race," that has a nice ring to it. It really does if it is indeed ready to race. Unfortunately most used racing cars aren't ready for much of anything other than restoration. Not all but a lot of them. We'll forego the horror stories. You'll get to hear enough stories from your racing buddies.

This is why we've been taking the time to observe. You have, hopefully, been going to races, deciding what class you want to run in, and you've been watching and sizing-up your future competition. In the class that you have chosen you have been studying all of the cars,

drivers, and teams. By now, you should know which ones are good, fast, and reliable. You have decided to buy one of them.

Now is the time to talk to the owner. Yes, he or she will sell it at the end of the season. The car has qualified for the regional (or national) run-offs. The car is fast and it has proven to be reliable. It has been well driven and the preparation has been meticulous. The driver will sell you the car as soon as the season's over. But he or she wants to clean it up first and make sure it is in good order after the last race. Great, you think. *Wrong!*

When the past driver gets out of that car at the end of its last race, take delivery on the spot. That is your insurance you are getting all of the goodies you are paying for. You'll have the whole winter break to clean the car, freshen the motor and the other bits that were worn during the last race, but it will all be there, just as it was last raced. If the driver blew it up or crashed it in the last race, you don't have to buy it, or maybe it will be a lot less money. That's up to you and the owner.

This process of picking out what car to buy is a real problem. Invest six months

SCCA club racing fields an interesting mix of cars from Corvettes to Datsun Z cars to Mazda RX-7s to an Alfa Romeo Alfetta GT, bringing up the rear.

or so going to a lot of races at different circuits. Talk to the competitors about their cars and about the others they compete against. Racers love to talk. Keep your eyes open and look. Watch how they drive, how they work on them, how they repair them, and how clean they keep them. Look for a driver who respects the car, tools, and the rest of the equipment. Look for the smooth driver who has the proper tools to care for the car—that's the one to buy from.

It's a good idea to take along someone who knows the cars and the classes, or a good racing mechanic to look at a potential car when you get to the point of really serious buying. Go to the owner's workshop and look it all over carefully, the car, the shop and the tools. If the car doesn't have good paint, interior, a sanitary engine compartment, and good clean wiring, then the car probably is deficient in a lot of other areas too. If the workshop is a mess, poorly lighted, and filthy, chances are so is the work done on the car. Let the buyer beware.

A serious and meticulous owner will have complete records on the car. Every race and testing lap that the car has run should have been recorded along with modifications, gearing, and speeds. Don't take everything the owner says for fact. Ask for proof. If he or she is honest, they will have no objections. Ask to see receipts; they can tell a lot. Take a look at the person selling the car. Would you buy a used car from them? Or better still would you want him or her to work on your race car? You'd better come up with the right answer on that one...he or she's been working on it for at least the last season. Remember, they are the one who wants to sell it. Why?

Take your time. There are a lot of race

It's better to have a first-class Showroom Stock car than a bare-boned Super-Vee with no spare parts. You can move into faster cars after you master the slower ones.

cars out there for sale and if one gets away there will always be another. Don't rush into something that you might regret later (if not immediately). Find the right one.

Safety Equipment

There's one more little detail that you'll have to take care of if you're going to race: safety equipment. Get the best you can afford; it can save your life. Don't cut corners here—or for that matter anywhere that can effect your safety. The better-quality equipment lasts longer, is safer, and offers the best protection. Before you buy anything, see what the other drivers (top drivers) are wearing. Find out what the SCCA and IMSA have on their approved lists.

I recommend one-piece driving suits, and full-face helmets with Nomex balaclavas, underwear, gloves, socks, and racing shoes. The more protection you can give yourself the safer you will be. In an enclosed car, the open-faced helmets are

The Simpson driving suit. One kind fits all, guys and gals.

still approved but a full-face Simpson is much safer—especially in the case of fire.

Again, the more you are protected the more you can concentrate on driving. Safe is sane, don't cut corners on safety equipment—buy the best. I recommend both Simpson helmets and driving suits, as well as their restraint systems.

More to think about? Don't worry, this is just the start. Once you get your race car you'll really have a lot to think about. Have you made any decisions yet? Made a deal to buy a car? Which one? This season's regional E-Production champion after he or she competes in the regional finale? Picking it up on the spot? Right,

you've been paying attention. It sounds like you're really getting into this in a big way.

How about what we just discussed? You've already enrolled in a Bondurant advanced class and you ran in the Barber series last summer, after the Bondurant Competition Road Racing course, and will be taking Bertil Roos' school in the spring. Great, by the time you start next season you really will be ready. You'll have all winter to prepare and test the car you are going to get after the finale. Important, testing and practice. Especially with a new car. There are a lot of other things you can do too, so keep on reading....

11

Getting a Sponsor

Let's assume your basic training was a success, you bought a reliable and competitive car, and have a season or two behind you with lots of victories and fastest laps. Even a few lap records for your class. All of your friends say, "You should go pro."

If you aspire to be a professional racer then you had better get the idea planted firmly in your head that *it is a serious and expensive business!* If you think it's not, then you are seriously mistaken.

The successful professional racer and the successful business person have a lot in common. What does it take to be successful? These attributes apply to both: Well-organized. Aggressive. Persistent. Competitive. Confident. Success oriented. Egotistical. Self-centered. Detail conscious. And have a positive attitude. Just the kind of person you'd want your brother or sister to marry? Not fantastically flattering but to the point. Of course, not all successful business people would make successful racers, but these days to be a successful racer you *must* be or learn to become successfully business oriented.

If you are serious about racing as a full-time career then you've just started to learn about what it takes. How you handle yourself off the track can be just as important as how you handle yourself on the track. You must now learn how to be a PR person. You need to be able to handle yourself well with the press, your sponsors, potential sponsors, car owners, crew, track personnel and every one else concerned with racing, especially the fans. Build a good following and give time to your supporters, they will be loyal, you must be too. You must give the media good interviews and learn how to provide your sponsors the best coverage (diplomatically) in all of your interviews—press, radio as well as television!

Perhaps the most important ingredient to your success (besides good driving and lots of money behind you) are good attitude, honesty and a pleasant personality. Be yourself, and be true to what you believe. You have to live with yourself first, so use integrity and you'll get along better with everyone else, too. A really important thing is to show all of that great en-

Let your enthusiasm for racing show!

thusiasm that you have. It's good for the media, your sponsors, racing in general and you personally. Some people hold it in. Don't—let it show! You'll get better coverage if you show it. That's what can make you or break you...that and cooperation.

Don't blame others or make excuses for your problems or mistakes, tell it like it is and you'll get a lot more respect, especially with the media. Also don't become a braggart—remember actions and results in a race car speak louder than words! It is a job, a great job, but still a job, so work at it. There are no free lunches.

As you turn professional you are going to find that it takes more than desire, more than talent and more than enthusiasm. Professional or amateur, it takes lots of hard work and a lot of money too. There aren't many of the "gentleman racers" left who have huge fortunes to spend on racing. Those guys now are mostly in Vintage

racing. It is another great segment of the sport and a fantastic time to be had by all, but not really a place for an up and coming professional. Today most first-class racing efforts are the result of large sponsor contributions and advertising dollars.

There's an old joke about how you can make a small fortune in motor racing: *Start with a large one.* Unfortunately in the current racing market, that is about the size of it. As racing becomes increasingly more expensive each season, the need for a driver to sell himself, his talent and his racing program to a sponsor or multiple sponsors is greater than ever.

You'll want to keep up on what is happening in the business world too. That's the only way you can make realistic proposals to sponsors. Find out what the sponsor's market needs are and try to fulfill them. Know which companies are having record profits, cash surpluses, opening new markets, or having record losses. Get familiar with *The Wall Street Journal*, *Business Week*, *Entrepreneur*, and the like. You really never know where a sponsor might come from. Some do it for direct marketing of their product or for advertising, others as a shelter from taxes. For others it is simply a means to entertain clients, friends and employees.

For an independent to run in anything beyond a club-type racing program without any sponsorship, and be competitive, is not too likely. You must have a good understanding of corporate needs, advertising and business practices as well as being able to *effectively present* and *communicate* to your sponsor. Just being a good driver doesn't cut it anymore. Sad but true. Major sponsorship is everywhere in professional racing. It is big business. Motor racing is a great advertising medium. Millions are spent on sponsorship.

The same financial needs are there for club racing too...only it's *you* who puts up the money for yourself and your car.

If you find a sponsor you are the lucky one. Help that person or company in any way you can. Give your sponsor his or her money's worth. Don't just take the money and ask for more when that runs out. There probably won't be more if you don't work with your sponsor. This goes right up the line all the way to Formula 1. It may require personal appearances, talk shows, radio, car shows, whatever. Maybe photos and personal meetings and dinners with your sponsor's clients and friends or other business contacts at a race meet or, whatever, wherever...do it.

If you don't have the time or know how to find a sponsor, then hire a good public relations firm or sponsor relations person. But remember, you still have to do

A well-heeled effort often requires the product and/or cash assistance of several sponsors—there are about a dozen logos displayed on this Porsche 935, which I co-drove to third place at Sebring in 1979. *Grand Prix Graphics*

Don't let the promotion work get you down—it can be a lot of fun too! That's me, without the bunny ears and tail, while on a Shelby PR tour in St. Louis. *ABK Photographic*

your part to keep the sponsor happy. Winning is important for the sponsor, but there are quite a few champions that have a terrible time keeping sponsors and lots of average drivers that always have a sponsor and many that have them a long time.

The sponsor needs results, true, but they also need a driver who will really work with them to accomplish their marketing goals. You have to retrain constant-ly to be good enough to win, but also you have to train just as hard at the public relations which your sponsor will need every bit as much. Give your team and your sponsor 110 percent.

Some World Champions are great to work with, and really go out of their way to look after the team sponsors. Others could care less. To some the sponsor is nothing more than a burden that needs to be around. One recent champion would regularly not show up for the sponsor's functions. The driver took the money but found little time for the sponsor's needs. That sponsor felt slighted and is no longer involved with motor racing.

This loss of sponsorship affected more than just that one selfish driver. The "It's not my problem" attitude affects everyone involved in racing. Sponsors are hard to get and when a sponsor is lost it is usually not regained...usually ever, by anyone.

Just don't forget, a good, friendly, positive and cooperative attitude goes a long way. If you find someone who has the faith in you and your talent to sponsor you, give them the help they need in return.

If you find a sponsor you are the lucky one. Help that person or company in any way you can. Give your sponsor his or her money's worth.

12

Take Some Tips From Me

You've been preparing your mind, your body, and your car, so what's next? Practice! Practice! Practice! My school helped to get you headed in the right direction, PROsearch gave you a real idea what competition is all about. You bought a good car and now you are learning the limits of both yourself and your car. That's what practice is all about. You will get better every time out. Remember: Safety, reliability, then performance—in that order. Now that it's time to practice, here are a few bits of information to help you on your way.

Practicing for Perfection

First, there is no such thing as too much practice. Unfortunately, when you're talking about practice you are also talking about a lot of time and money. Practice doesn't mean just driving around the track. That's what a lot of people do but that's not what I'm talking about. The *quality* of time spent practicing is perhaps more important than the amount of time spent. Make each lap count. Really con-

centrate and feel exactly what your car is doing.

Most tracks are available to groups or individuals to rent, but it's expensive, so spend your time fruitfully. Don't pay your practice fee and sit there and work on your car all day long, hardly turning a wheel. You can do that in your garage. Work on your car in your garage and have everything ready to drive when you arrive at the track. Don't waste your time and your money. Arrive at the track with your car well-prepared and ready to race (or practice)...just like a race weekend!

Even before you think about going to a track to practice, have in mind what you want to accomplish. Do you want to improve a basic or special technique; your car's handling; see how a new part works or doesn't work? Know what you want to do. Every lap costs you money. Even if nothing breaks it will cost you in car and tire wear. So, make sure you are going to get your money's worth.

Preparation is the key to both successful practice and successful racing. Your car must be meticulously prepared and be as safe as theoretically possible to enable you to get the most out of your practice, testing, qualifying, or racing. Don't make excuses for yourself why you can't do something. Just do it or don't run.

Warming Up Yourself and Your Car

There is actually one little step past preparation that will really make a difference as to how you and your car perform: Warm-up! *Warm-up is an absolute necessity.* An athlete, say a runner, wouldn't consider starting a race cold. He or she would get injured, strain something, or just wouldn't perform up to what they could if all of their muscles were warm and ready to go.

The same thing applies to a car, on the street or on the track. Warm-up is imperative. By this I don't mean let the car idle for a few minutes then take off hard. By warm up I mean a complete warm up. Think of it like this: In the morning when you first wake up you might be a little slow and sluggish till you have your shower and your exercise or your morning coffee. It just takes a few minutes to get yourself going, before you're functioning up to par.

Your car has to wake up gradually, too. There are parts that take a little more time to get ready than others. The engine is usually the first thing to warm up. But then what? You probably haven't even thought about it. Now's the time.

Warm the engine at a medium idle before you do anything else. This will give you a lot more time to think, relax, and plan before you get underway. When the water temperature moves into the operating range you're ready to start out. Don't forget, right now the only thing that's warmed up is the engine, so take it easy. The wheel bearings, transmission, differential oil, and the gears are all still cold. In Formula 1, they warm up the gearbox with the car jacked up and in gear, running to help bring everything up to temperature. They heat the tires to bring them to a proper operating temperature too. Probably the thing that most people forget is the tires. If they are not up to working temperature you're going to fly right off the road from lack of grip.

Take it easy on the track, make sure everything is warm and ready to go, espe-

Many students bring their own cars for my course. This Porsche 914 is way too wide of the apex area, which is marked by the pylons.

cially your tires. Give it a couple laps at a slow and safe speed before you put it to the floor. On the street, give your car a few miles to get everything warm. Getting all of the parts warmed up will really minimize the wear and dramatically increase the life of your car. You'll have far fewer failures and it will perform a lot better for a lot longer. For peak performance both you and your car need that extra little bit of easy warm up. Be gentle with it. Just give yourself that extra few minutes for preparation; it'll maximize your potential and in the long run everything will work better and longer. Don't forget, racetrack or street, high-performance driving is knowing what you and your car are doing all of the time.

Be sure that the running gear, shock absorbers, and tires are warmed up too. The tires are, for safety reasons, the most important things to have at working temperature. If they are not warm enough before you really get into it then there is little adhesion...and it's into the weeds! If you remember the 1992 Indy 500, the temperature was cold and the tires had a problem in heating up. The pole sitter spun out on the pace lap and there were numerous crashes, almost one after each caution. Almost every time they restarted, the tires were cold from following the pace car and someone else would spin or crash.

A lot depends on the car you are driving. A formula car will take longer to warm up than a sports car or sedan simply because it weighs so much less. Also, the harder the tire compound, the slower it is to warm up. If the temperature is really cold or the track damp it will take even longer to bring your tires up to optimum operating temperature, maybe a couple of laps—so don't rush it.

Choosing High-Performance Tires

What about tires...all of the manufacturers claim theirs are the best, so what are you going to choose? If you are asking about a street car, showroom stocker or a racer that must use a stock treaded tires then you've got a lot to choose from. Read the reports in *Road & Track, Car and Driver, Motor Trend, Autoweek*, and the like. Also, talk to different people with the same kind of car. Try to drive several cars to find out what the different tires work like. Your dilemma then becomes a process of elimination.

For racing in the United States, the novice or national racer is probably best off with Goodyear. That's what most of the competition will be using. If you're running the same tires as your competition and they are just as new and you're running the same tire pressure, then you've just eliminated a variable in how your car handles in comparison to the competition. The more variables you can eliminate the quicker you'll be able to set up and dial in your car. For the proper rates of inflation, check with your tire representative at the event—one more reason to choose Goodyear.

For the street, tire choices are numerous. As I said, do your homework, spend time on research. What kind of tread? What kind of tire? The technology of tire development is constantly changing. Constantly getting better. There will always be better, stickier tires, for the street and for the track. Keep on top of it by reading, listening and researching and, if possible, testing. Tire wear and tire life are a definite consideration if you are on a limited budget. The latest up-to-date new tires are usually the best and the quickest. I use Goodyears on all of my cars because they are the best.

Tire consumption at the Bondurant School is always a major financial consideration, as it is with any racer. Goodyear Eagle high-performance racing and GT tires give our students maximum performance, adhesion and safety with a minimum of tire wear. They really perform great for all of our needs.

As for racing with street GT tires, I would recommend having the treads shaved off by your tire distributor to increase their adhesion as well as their life under racing conditions. Some are being manufactured now, already shaved, just for racing.

Tire Temperatures and Inflation Rates

Tire temperatures should be monitored every time you come into the pits. It will give you a definite clue as to what your car is or isn't doing. Your tire rep will be able to tell you how and where to check the temps and what they mean. The temperature will vary from the center to the edges of the tire, depending on how you have your car set up. It can also tell you what part of the tire is working and what part isn't due to your suspension set.

The inflation rates and types of compound to use on a given day are other bits of information you want to talk over with your tire company technical engineer. They will be of as much help as possible since it's to their advantage to see you do well. That's what they are there for and part of what you paid for when you bought those expensive skins.

The same goes for wet-weather tires. Talk to your tech rep and use the information that is available to you.

For all forms of driving, tire pressure is really important. Keep your tires properly inflated. I recommend 35psi as a starting point. I intend to drive my high-perfor-

mance cars fast and hard, so I push my tire pressures up a bit above the manufacturer's recommended pressures. At my school I run all of the cars at 40psi all the way around. It's a real safety factor.

When street tires (on most street wheels) are run at or below normal inflation rates the tire bead can break under hard cornering, the tire casing can roll over and come off the rim or lose air rapidly. If it comes off while you're really pushing it hard in a corner, the wheel rim edge will dig into the pavement and you could be in for a really big accident, maybe even a rollover.

Like the rest of your car, keep your tires in top condition and properly inflated. They are your only contact with the road surface! If you have treaded tires, make sure that you have enough tread.

Be sure they are in proper balance too, on the street or the race track. Not only will a good balancing prolong their life but it will reduce high-speed vibrations. Properly balanced tires reduce the chance of hot spots, overheating, and blistering, which can prevent a blow-out.

Shock Absorbers and Anti-Sway Bars

In addition to your tires you must concern yourself with your shock absorbers and anti-sway bars. On my school cars, I use stiffer springs and larger-diameter sway bars than stock as well as Koni adjustable shocks. There are many kinds of shocks, springs, and anti-sway bars available on the market so it's time for you to determine just which are the best for you.

One of the fastest and most efficient ways to determine the set-up is to contact a competition suspension specialist. They can give you the best set-up for the kind of driving that you want to do with your particular car. If you want it for the street, it should be a little softer ride than for a full-race set-up. You don't want it so stiff that you rattle your brains. Each kind of driving has different handling requirements. Setting up your car for the street is far different from setting up for a slalom, autocross, rally, or improved touring race set-up. Each requires a different kind of suspension setting and geometry so you'd be best off to contact a suspension specialist to design one for your car, your driving style, and your specific needs.

Setting an Engine Red-Line

Once you've decided on the specific areas you want to work on and have properly warmed up your car and your tires, you should pick a predetermined engine red-line and stick to it. (You've just eliminated another variable in setting up your car.) This should remain constant so you can gauge improvement accordingly. Run fast enough to find out what the car will do and spot the changes, but be sure to shift at the red-line so that it won't damage your engine.

Forget about your speedometer, it's not important. What is important is how many revs you are turning. That should be your concern, not your top speed. Some racers disconnect the speedometer so that they aren't preoccupied with it.

Of all your instruments your tachometer is one of the most important and should be checked two or three times a lap and especially see what your "tattle-tale" marker is reaching. The seasoned racer becomes accustomed to listening to the engine sound and that reads quite accurately to the tach. But until you can do that perfectly, check your tach. Who knows, you might be short shifting by 500 or 1000rpm.

Be sure to check all of your instruments a few times a lap. When it is safe and you can relax your concentration momentarily. It's best to pick a couple spots on a longish straightaway to give them a quick glance. That quick glance at your oil-pressure and oil-temperature and water-temperature gauges will let you know if you have problems on the way. They can save you lots of money, so use them!

How to Test and Practice

While testing and practicing, don't spend too many laps on the track without

Choose a couple of spots on each lap to quickly check all of your gauges. The banking at Daytona is an example of a good spot; just cruising along, in 1965, at about 200+ mph. Not much else to do but read the needles. *Dave Friedman*

a break or you'll find yourself making the same mistakes time after time. Eight or ten laps are usually a good number to run at one time. Then, come in and figure out what you've been doing right or wrong. Get out of the car and really think about it. Isolate what you did right and what you did wrong; find ways to improve when you go out again. Isolate where you could be smoother, faster, more consistent. Did you hit your apex areas right? How about your downshifts? Are you trailing your brake properly and long enough? Is your chassis set properly through the corners? Are you braking late enough or hard enough? Did you really blow a couple of corners?

Your perspective really changes once you've stepped out of the car. Once back in the car, before you go out again, close your eyes and imagine every corner, every straightaway, just like it really is. Picture a perfect lap and then get out there and do it.

During each lap in practice, think how and where you can go quicker. Check the tach as you exit the corners to see if you're really quicker or if it just felt like you were. Remember, smooth is quick, so be as smooth as you can. If you make a mistake, correct it as best you can, smoothly, then put it aside until you've finished that session. When you are behind the wheel, think about where you are going, not where you have been.

One word about practicing braking. Most novice drivers don't realize how deep they can brake into a corner driving a race car. This is something that you must learn. The best way to practice this is to find a hard 90degree corner or a hairpin with a lot of run-off room, where a spin won't be dangerous. Each time you approach the corner try braking a little later

The information from section timing is valuable data that clearly shows the worth of modifications to your car or your technique.

and a little later until you reach the point where you start to lock up your brakes because you are about to overshoot your turn-in point. You now know how deep you can go before you have to brake.

When you practice your braking, don't forget the basics: Lightly double-pump, then squeeze on your brake pedal so you can feel what your brakes are doing, finish your major braking, and continue trail-braking into the first third of the corner, slowly easing off to keep weight on your front tires in order to maintain the chassis set, then ease on the throttle. It's simple, once you know how deep you can go into a turn before braking. You should be able to figure out just about any corner without looping it if you know how much distance it takes to brake from what speed.

Don't forget to try to use alternate lines on some corners just to see what will happen if you are forced to use them under racing conditions. No matter what it is that you are working at to improve or test, be sure to do it completely and methodically with your full concentration. You really must concentrate fully 100 percent of the time. You'll increase your confidence as well as your ability. Your marked progress and quicker lap times will definitely help you to build enthusiasm and self-assurance.

If you have some friends or family that can give you a hand on your test days and at the races, they can help you make better use of your time by videotaping you and section timing, like at the entry and exit of a difficult corner to see how you progress. Another option is to mount a small video camera on your rollbar during your race or practice. This really helps when you review what you did and where and why. Just as pro football players re-

view their game tapes, a video system will give you the benefit of being able to see, on the spot, the replay of what you are doing right and what you are doing wrong. From reviewing these tapes you can immediately begin working on the problems.

Having a friend time you through specific corners or sections as you experiment with different braking points, variation in you racing lines and other changes in your car, can be useful too. Even though you may have the same tach reading at the exit of the corner, one line might be slightly quicker than another and you might carry more speed down the following straight. With section timing this can be readily seen.

Another possibility is to tape and time your competition (those faster, not slower, than you) in the same sections you do yourself, then compare. It will help you become more competitive with them by seeing what they do right, wrong, or just different as compared to yourself. Especially watch how they make passes on other cars. This is one area that makes some drivers nervous, as it is up to the overtaking driver to make a clean pass. Watch how the best do it and it will help you too. *The better you know your competition the better you will do against them.*

Another thing, please try not to be just a dry-weather driver. If it is raining, go for it anyway. Lots of drivers pack it up and leave for home at the sign of the first rain. Practice is practice! Road races are also run in the rain so you'd better practice in the rain, too. Get used to it, if you really want to become a good driver. It doesn't mean you have to like it, just get good at it. Besides, driving in the wet is a fantastic way to learn more. You really have to be

You can learn a lot from practicing in the rain. Wet conditions are a fact of life in this sport—especially in England. Here I am in Sid Taylor's McLaren at Silverstone in 1966. I finished second behind Denny Hulme.

smoother, gentler, concentrate harder, and be even more precise at controlling your car in wet conditions.

In the wet you are going at a lot slower speed and you can really experience less traction and faster responses from your car. You reach the limit of adhesion much faster and you force yourself to improve your concentration and reaction speed. The wet forces you to be a much smoother driver; so take advantage of the rain, and practice, you'll be amazed at how much you can learn. You'll end up being quicker in the dry from it, too.

As far as practice goes, practice all of the time. Every time you are behind the wheel, practice—on the street or track, practice something. Like I said before, use your head, be careful, don't jeopardize anyone else, and take it easy on the street.

Driving on the street is a good place to practice smoothness, concentration, heel-and-toe downshifting, and other basic techniques that you'll need on the racetrack, but don't have to go fast to practice. If you practice and perfect them on the street, then when you're on the track you can concentrate on the other aspects of racing, like testing and learning to go quicker.

Testing is practice, true. But, although you're combining all the basics you learned from practice, you're also now starting to develop your car. Once you've got yourself dialed in, now is the time for your car.

Rule #1: Only change one thing at a time!
Rule #2: Record each change made and it's effect and result.

Rule #3: Time every lap—always: practicing, testing, and racing.

Rule #4: Keep a record of times and changes for each circuit you run.

All of this should save you time and make your testing more productive. Try to be able to test at a session apart from a race meet. You'll have more time and be more efficient. Then, when you come to race qualifying, you'll do much better.

A word about Rule #1: If you have a handling problem, take each change as a separate thing. It may be your tire pressure, your shock absorber setting or your anti-rollbar adjustment. Just change one thing at a time. Find out if the change makes it better or worse before you make another change. Record each change and its effect before you move on to the next change and work that one out. It's a process of elimination. Do it orderly, for the best results. If you change three or four adjustments at once, you won't know which one made it better or worse.

Maybe your problem isn't mechanical, maybe it's you and what you are doing. Some problems are really solved simply. Use your head and run about eight or ten laps, then get out of the car and think about what you've been doing. Really analyze.

A Corvette driver I knew was having trouble with his brakes one race meet. It was an important national race and he was under pressure to do well. But he wasn't thinking. He reported to his crew that his brakes were pulling hard to the right at the end of two long and fast straightaways. His crew spent hours trying

See you at the races!

to find the brake problem and couldn't find anything wrong, but kept trying to correct the problem. It wasn't the brakes...it was him. He was pushing so hard on the brakes to slow the big 'vette that he was accidentally pulling up on the steering wheel for leverage. The car wasn't pulling right under braking; it was being *steered* to the right without him realizing it. Use your head; analyze what you are doing and you'll do just fine.

Whatever your racing choice, it takes a lot of time behind the wheel to perfect it. Give a lot of thought to the different kinds of racing available to you. They're all good practice. Karts, midgets, sprint cars, stockers—all of them will give you experience and that's what is necessary when you're starting out. Most of the current Formula 1 drivers started out in karts. It's fast and competitive and, like motorcycles, it teaches you to get used to having competitors close around you. Whatever you can drive on a track is better than not racing at all. Practice with them the same as you would in a real race. Do eight or ten laps then get out and think about it. When you do your next eight or ten laps a few minutes later you'll be quicker.

Well, you're just about on your own now. I hope you listened and think about what you're doing. Take your time and do it right. Practice, practice, practice to per-fect it and read, read, read. Read everything you can about driving, racing, car preparation, and the rules. Read the business section of the paper as well as the classified ads in addition to the auto and racing publications. Everything has clues—learn to read and interpret them. Give yourself a broad base of knowledge and you'll have a lot more information and experience to draw from.

In our final section on sources you'll get a full list of recommended reading, schools and publications as well as some companies that can provide you with good information on what they are doing for racing and can do for you.

I hope you get along well in your quest for racing. Remember: Put yourself on a rigorous training program; lay out a promotional and sponsorship package; run your racing program like the business it is; give yourself a plan for the racing goals you want to achieve; practice any chance you can.

Put together all that talent that you have and use it to the fullest. It's not going to be easy, but it is great when you achieve your goals. Work out a long-term and a short-term plan to get you headed in the right direction. All the best of luck to you and keep in touch. See you at the races!

Sources

Driving Schools

Bob Bondurant School of High Performance
    Driving
Firebird International Raceway
20000 S. Maricopa Road, Gate #3
Chandler, Arizona 85226
P.O. Box 51980
Phoenix, Arizona 85076
Info: 1-800-842-7223
Tele: (602) 796-1111
FAX: (602) 796-0660

Bertil Roos Grand Prix Racing School
Pocco International Raceway
P.O. Box 221
Blakeslee, PA 18610
Tele: 1-800-RACE-NOW

Russell Racing School
11023 Monterey Hwy.
Salinas, CA 93908
Tele: (408) 372-7223
FAX: (408) 372-0458

Elf Winfield/Franam Racing, Inc.
Circuit Paul Ricard
Le Castelet, France
1409 South Wilshire Drive
Minnetonka, MN 55343
Tele: (612) 541-9461

Bobby Rahal's Track Time
4600-A Middle Drive
Youngstown, OH 44505
Tele: (216) 759-1868

NASTRACK
(Richard Petty's Driving School)
1150 Ivey Cline
Concord, NC 28027
Tele: (704) 784-8310
FAX: (704) 784-8601

Jim Russell Racing Drivers School
Le Circuit Mont-Tremblant
P.O. Box 119
Mont-Tremblant
Quebec, Canada J0T 1Z0
Tele: (819) 425-2739
FAX: (819) 425-9183

Jim Russell Racing School
Donnington Park
England
Tele: (0332) 811430

Skip Barber Racing School
(Eastern Headquarters)
Route 7
Canaan, CT 06018
Tele: (203) 824-0771

(Western Headquarters)
Sears Point International Raceway
29355 Arnold Drive
Sonoma, CA 95476
Tele: (707) 939-8000

Drive Tech Racing School
2344 West Saratoga Way
San Bernadino, California 92407
Tele: (202) 833-9133

Bell Helmets/Racestar
15301 Shoemaker Ave.
Norwalk, CA 90650

Ford Motor Company
Ford Special Vehicle Operations
North American Automotive Operations
17000 Southfield Road
Allen Park, Michigan 48101

Goodyear Tire Corporation
1144 E. Market Street
Akron, Ohio 44316

KeiperRecaro
905 West Maple Road, Suite 100
Clawson, MI 48017

Koni America
ITT Automotive
8085 Production Avenue
Florence, Kentucky 41041

RaceMark Driving Suits
RaceMark Manufacturing
P.O. Box 1089
Schenectady, New York 12301

Ronal Wheels
15692 Computer Lane
Huntington Beach, California 92649

Safety Devices Inc. U.S.A. (Roll Bars)
15 Central Way
Department 300
Kirkland, Washington 98033

Simpson Safety Equipment
2415 Amsler
Torrance, California 90505

Books

Many of the following recommended books
    are available from:
Motorbooks International
P.O. Box 1
Osceloa, WI 54020
1-800-826-6600

Competition Driving, by Alain Prost with
    Jean Pierre Rousselot. Motorbooks
    International.

Engineer to Win, by Carroll Smith.
    Motorbooks International.

Formula Car Technology, by Hody Holmes.
    Steve Smith Autosports Publications.

Prepare to Win, by Carroll Smith. Aero Pub-
    lishers, Inc.

Racing Car Design and Development, by Len
    Terry and Alan Baker. Robert Bentley,
    Inc.

The Art and Science of Grand Prix Driving,
    by Niki Lauda. Motorbooks International.

The Racing Driver, by Denis Jenkinson.

The Techniques of Motor Racing, by Piero
    Taruffi.

Tune to Win, by Carroll Smith. Aero Publish-
    ers, Inc.

Superdriver, by Sir John Whitmore. Motor-
    books International.

Index